Presidential Transactions

Presidential Transactions

Robert J. Sickels
University of New Mexico

Prentice-Hall, Inc. Englewood Cliffs, New Jersey

Library of Congress Cataloging in Publication Data

SICKELS, ROBERT J
    Presidential transactions.

    Includes bibliographical references.
    1. Presidents—United States. I. Title.
JK516.S5   353.03'13   73–11012
ISBN 0–13–697888–6
ISBN 0–13–697870–3 (pbk.)

Printed in the United States of America

Prentice-Hall International, Inc., *London*
Prentice-Hall of Australia, Pty. Ltd., *Sydney*
Prentice-Hall of Canada, Ltd., *Toronto*
Prentice-Hall of India Private Limited, *New Delhi*
Prentice-Hall of Japan, Inc., *Tokyo*

1787803

For My Father

Contents

Introduction

In this study the insights of exchange theory are applied to an old, familiar, and still largely mysterious institution, the American presidency, to reveal primary patterns of presidential behavior and to dispel some of the mystery. The basic assumption of exchange theory is that people calculate their own interests rationally, and act on those calculations. In this view of human behavior, political as well as economic interactions depend upon mutual expectations of gain. Participants in the political system engage in exchanges if, and only if, they believe that they stand to profit.[1] As one of the participants, the president calculates probable costs and benefits in transactions with party leaders, congressmen, judges, and others, and makes his decisions to exchange or not; and other participants make similar decisions about whether to deal with the president. This perspective helps to explain the frustration and loneliness that presidents have experienced in office for want of the political currency to buy the cooperation of certain powerful figures in the political system, and some of the tendencies toward presidential autocracy.

Exchange analysis is not the usual approach to the study of political behavior. Rational self-interest is assumed to be the basis of some other kinds of common activities, such as buying and selling, but in politics it is widely regarded as an aberration. Most writers on politics and the presidency avoid the assumptions of exchange theory altogether. Historians and biographers do most of the best work on the presidency without this or any other theoretical framework. Constitutionalists, emphasizing the powers of the office, see the presidency as a conjunction of opportunities and constraints broadly defined by law, subject to the interpretations of the president and the other branches of government. To many political scientists, political leadership is a matter of manipulation. In *Presidential Power* Richard Neustadt seems to say that a shrewd president will have his way with other members of the political system, an explanation that is tempting in the light of Watergate disclosures.

Each of these approaches has its value, and each has some limitations that exchange analysis helps to correct. Historians and biographers stress the unique over the recurrent, while exchange analysis is attuned to general explanation. In an age of discretionary government particularly, constitutionalists may overestimate the influence of written rules on official behavior. Students of manipulative politics who, in the Machiavellian tradition, emphasize the skills of leadership, tend to see presidents as heroes or ne'er-do-wells, and ignore objective constraints that even the most skillful incumbent cannot overcome. Exchange analysis encourages realistic generalization about the problems presidents have in establishing or maintaining close relationships with other parts of the political system, while pointing out equally well the conditions of warm cooperation.

In the following chapters we shall examine the transactions of presidents (and in some instances presidential candidates) with party members, advisors, bureaucrats, judges, congressmen, and members of the general public. In each, normal patterns of exchange are distinguished from those that are more intense or less intense. Every effort has been made to avoid the dual errors of letting facts speak for themselves and forcing them unnaturally into a formal framework: special features in each relationship are noted, and behavior that cannot be explained as self-interest—a president acting on principle alone, or by impulse, for example—is noted. It is enough that exchange analysis explain a good deal; it need not attempt to explain everything.

The lawlessness uncovered by the Watergate investigations is unprecedented—not "politics as usual," as a majority of Americans are known to have believed at the time. Much of it defies explanation. Personal enrichment from public funds is not unknown in American politics, it is true, although most presidents have overcome that temptation. Some precedent can be found, too, for manipulation of the news and attacks on the press by the White House. For electoral corruption of the magnitude of 1972 one must go back as far as the theft of the presidential election of 1876.

But there is no precedent for secret political police in the White House, for a presidential order to mobilize the civilian and military intelligence establishment for surveillance of political opponents, or for presidential endorsement of the opening of mail, electronic eavesdropping, burglary, and other unlawful behavior (described in the secret Huston Report to the president in 1970) as a regular part of the political process.[2] Together with a determined evasion of congressional checks on policy, spending, appointments, and conduct of the war, these developments suggest that a coup d'etat was set in motion, from above, during the presidency of Richard Nixon.[3]

Our tradition of constitutional democracy is in jeopardy when power collects in the hands of a few political leaders who hold themselves above the law. The Watergate scandals were the work of men estranged from the political system. Now, particularly, in the aftermath of Watergate, it is important to recall the American tradition, the full complexity of its transactions, and its insistence upon the sharing of political power.

Notes

[1]See Peter Blau, *Exchange and Power in Social Life* (New York: John Wiley & Sons, Inc. 1964); R. L. Curry and L. L. Wade, *A Theory of Political Exchange* (Englewood Cliffs, N.J.: Prentice-Hall, Inc., 1968); William C. Mitchell, "The Shape of Political Theory to Come: From Political Sociology to Political Economy," in *Politics and the Social Sciences* ed. Seymour M. Lipset (New York: Oxford University Press, Inc., 1969), pp. 101–36; Anthony Downs, *An Economic Theory of Democracy* (New York: Harper & Row, Publishers, 1957), particularly the discussion of self-interest in Chap. 2.

[2]*New York Times,* June 7, 1973, p. 36.

[3]Malcolm Moos in the *New York Times,* June 8, 1973, p. 39.

**O
n
e** The President
and
His
Party

Compared with most political parties here and abroad, the Democrats and the Republicans in the United States are unfeigningly business-like. Their business is political office and the rewards of office. Undistracted by questions of philosophy and ideology, the parties compete to nominate and elect their leaders in season, and rest when the season is over.

To enter upon a discussion of the presidency with the period of nomination and election is not only convenient, taking first things first, it is particularly instructive in an exchange analysis of the presidency, because here the calculations posited by the exchange model are clearest and purest. Legal, moral, and customary considerations prevail at times in transactions of the president and other components of the political system, but in the dealings of parties and presidential candidates, hard and straightforward bargaining is usual.

Normal Exchange
between President and Party

To become president one must engage in exchanges with enough primary voters and convention delegates to be nominated, and with enough voters in November to be elected. The party members—the voters and their local, state, and national organizations, leaving aside for the moment the members of Congress—support a candidate during the nomination and election process in anticipation of reward when he becomes president. A condition of this exchange is the candidate's and the party's desire for a victory in November: the party looks for a winning candidate—Sherman Adams backed Eisenhower for the Republican nomination because he "looked like the fastest horse in the stable"[1]—and the candidate, once nominated, seeks a winning electoral coalition.

For the candidate, the attractiveness of the presidency is self-evident. For the members of the party the rewards vary; some are distributed widely, some narrowly. Party members at large benefit if their candidate wins, objectively in the implementation of policy, subjectively in the satisfaction of watching the team win and having one's own in the White House. A smaller group of party regulars hope for patronage—jobs, contracts, and other favors.

Even more narrowly, fellow partisans on the ballot with the candidate for president hope to be elected to office on his coattails. Those planning to run later in his term count on campaign assistance in the form of money, endorsement, and personal appearances in return for their electoral support. But since the impact of a presidential candidate or a president on lesser elections is unpredictable, it is a minor exchange. Republican experience in the last generation illustrates the risks. Despite the great popularity of Dwight Eisenhower, the voters did not return a Republican majority to Congress mid-term in 1954, and they reelected him in 1956, as they did Richard Nixon in 1972, with a Democratic Congress. Before his election to the presidency, Richard Nixon had gained a reputation for vigorous campaigning on behalf of Republican candidates—working harder for the presidential candidate in 1964 than the candidate himself—but when he led the Republican ticket in 1968, there was no coattail effect.[2] In 1972 Nixon made little effort to help fellow candidates. Some in the party said that his aloofness from the campaign cost the election of Republicans on the ballot with him. The expectation of campaign assistance is a small part of the typical electoral exchange.

What has been said so far holds true in most cases, but not in all, to be sure. Sometimes members of a party seek benefits that do not rest on an assumption of the presidential candidate's electoral victory. Some party members and leaders may quite rationally prefer the defeat of their presidential candidate to a victory threatening their control of the party machinery. Many moderate and liberal Republicans hoped for the defeat of Barry Goldwater in 1964, for example, and many moderate and conservative Democrats hoped for the defeat of George McGovern in 1972. In each case four more years of the other party in the White House seemed preferable to the loss of the organization to an ideologically exclusive minority. Another segment of the public not devoted to winning are the members of small political parties of the left and the right, such as the Socialist party of Eugene Debs and Norman Thomas earlier in the century, or the American party in 1972, which nominated a member of the John Birch Society for president. Functionally such organizations are more like pressure groups than parties.

Most party members and most candidates for the presidency, however, are interested in the fruits of victory. They exchange electoral support for benefits from election day on. In this framework, the candidate's problem is to construct a coalition to win the nomination and another to win the November election. It is a task complicated by an electoral system which distorts popular support at each stage in the selection of a president. In exchange terms the electoral value of the support of a given number of people in the nomination and in the election is predictable only within broad tolerances.

The Nomination of a President

In nominating a presidential candidate, the party normally attempts to select someone who seems likely to win the general election. A serious contender for the nomination must demonstrate that he stands a good chance of defeating the candidate of the other party. But unless he has won a presidential election before, the party has uncertain information, at best, about his appeal in a contest with a known or an unknown opponent. Ultimately the national convention must decide, relying heavily on the candidates' standings in the preference primaries for predictions of their performance in the general election.

The selection of a good candidate is hazardous and exciting because of the unreliability of primary results. Presidential primaries were originally expected to reduce the uncertainties of the nominating process, but they rarely do. One reason is that some contenders have no primary record. In 1960 John Kennedy needed primary victories to prove that people would vote for a Catholic for president, but Lyndon Johnson thought it prudent to avoid the primaries and appeal to the convention directly. Another problem is that a primary record is always a doubly unrepresentative sample of party opinion. In each state the members of the party who vote in the primary are qualitatively different from those who vote in the general election.[3] And in entering primaries where he thinks he can do well, the candidate deliberately avoids unfriendly segments of the party membership. Whatever the reasons for the selection of primaries in an election year, they are not a proper sample of the national mood. The key primary for John Kennedy in 1960 was in heavily Protestant, poor, rural West Virginia. In 1968 another small state had an extraordinary impact on the nomination, when Eugene McCarthy ran neck and neck with Lyndon Johnson in the New Hampshire primary and set off a chain of events that included the entry of Robert Kennedy into the race, President Johnson's announcement that he would not seek reelection, and, ultimately, the defeat of Hubert Humphrey in the general election.

The 1968 Democratic experience in New Hampshire illustrates a third uncertainty in primary results. Although Senator McCarthy's unexpected showing was almost universally taken as an expression of criticism of President Johnson's enlargement of the war in Vietnam, public opinion polls made it clear—a year later, when the analysis was published in an obscure journal—that the voters had meant no such thing. Despite the clarity of the senator's position on the war, there were more who favored a tougher war policy among those who voted for him, in fact, than who favored withdrawal. By a narrow margin, those who had supported Senator McCarthy in the spring preferred George Wallace to Hubert Humphrey or Richard Nixon in November.[4]

A fourth trouble with primaries is that the candidates prejudice the results by self-serving prognostications and postmortems. Since it is commonly supposed that a primary victory depends not so much on gaining a large plurality or even a small one as on doing better than expected, a contender assumes the dual task of maximizing votes and minimizing public expectations. He may emphasize one or the other. Thus, if he seems unlikely to win a healthy plurality, a candidate will try to convince the press and the public that he is impoverished, far from home and friends, in a state with unique problems, and too busy with important duties elsewhere to campaign effectively, and that he will be grateful for a modest tally against an opponent who has many advantages, fair and otherwise. If he thinks he will do well, however, the candidate will characterize the primary as a difficult but faithful test of his strength as a presidential contender.

Then it is up to the convention to select a likely winner. The delegates watch all signs, including the results of the primaries. To the distortions of the primaries, however, the convention adds its own. It is, inevitably, skewed in favor of a candidate or a region. In 1912 the Republican convention was apportioned in a way that gave the South many more delegates than their share of party membership. President

Taft was renominated with southern support in a contest with Theodore Roosevelt, the more popular candidate among the voters. Roosevelt bolted the Republican party, ran as a third-party candidate, and came in second behind the Democrat, Woodrow Wilson, in the general election. Taft ran a poor third, carrying only Utah and Vermont. In 1972 the convention that renominated Richard Nixon also fixed the apportionment of the 1976 convention in a way that favored the smaller states and, many conservative delegates hoped, the nomination of Vice-President Agnew for president.

Within each state the process of selecting delegates introduces another bias in popular representation. The traditional winner-take-all plan allows the leading factions of a state and its districts to win most or all of the delegates. The quota system tried by Democrats in many states in 1972 made the national convention more representative of youth, women, and blacks than it had been before, but less representative of Democrats as a whole, proving that the broadest solution has not yet been found. And even if a convention's plan of representation were relatively equitable, there would always be credentials fights, the last-minute jockeying and bullying to bend the rules to allow the seating of delegates whose right to sit is unclear. In some conventions contests over the seating of disputed delegations tip the balance of the convention to one side or the other. Dwight Eisenhower's nomination was assured in the Republican convention of 1952 when his forces won a procedural vote barring contested delegates who had not received the support of at least two-thirds of the national committee from voting on the credentials of others. George McGovern's nomination in the Democratic convention of 1972 turned upon a similar ruling, from the chair, that contested delegates would not vote on their own seating and that the majority required to decide a seating contest in the convention would be reduced accordingly.

What is astounding is that, distortions of primaries and conventions notwithstanding, the typical outcome is the selection of a contender who is likely to put up a good fight in November—Eisenhower's selection over "Mr. Republican," Robert Taft, whom polls showed to be considerably less popular among the voters, is a case in point. Senator McGovern's nomination, as we shall see, is one of the rare departures from the rule. If the convention is deadlocked, the nominee may be a compromise candidate who is the first choice of few but second choice of many and, under the circumstances, the rational alternative. In the Republican convention of 1920, Warren Harding emerged as a "dark horse" candidate after two days of balloting failed to give either of the two leading contenders a majority. During the night, enough party leaders agreed on Harding to give him the nomination and the next day he was chosen by the convention.

What makes the selection of Harding particularly interesting is the way it followed a script written by Harding's manager, Harry Daugherty, months before the convention. Harding would be chosen in a "smoke-filled room," he predicted, after the delegates had tried and failed to name other candidates. He said, "I don't expect Senator Harding to be nominated on the first, second, or third ballots, but I think we can afford to take chances that, about eleven minutes after two, Friday morning of the convention, when ten or twenty weary men are sitting around a table, someone will say, 'Who will we nominate?' At that decisive time the friends of Harding will suggest him and can well afford to abide by the result."[5] Daugherty's forecast missed the hour, but he described the fateful meeting in the Blackstone Hotel accurately in all other respects.

The American political parties' preoccupation with picking winners has brought some criticism. At the end of the last century the English historian James Bryce, in a chapter of his work, *The American Commonwealth,* entitled "Why Great Men Are Not Chosen Presidents," wrote:

> Europeans often ask ... how it happens that this great office ... is not more frequently filled by great and striking men?
>
> ... Eminent men make more enemies, and give those enemies more assailable points, than obscure men do. They are therefore in so far less desirable candidates. ... Hence, when the choice lies between a brilliant man and a safe man, the safe man is preferred. Party feeling, strong enough to carry in on its back a man without conspicuous positive merits, is not always strong enough to procure forgiveness for a man with positive faults.
>
> "B" (so reason the leaders), "who is one of our possible candidates, may be an abler man than A, who is the other. But we have a better chance of winning with A than with B, while X, the candidate of our opponents, is anyhow no better than A. We must therefore run A."[6]

Another Englishman, Harold Laski, writing during the New Deal, dissented from this view. His answer to Bryce was

> ... first, that many first-rate men have become president by reason of the system; and second, that the reasons which stopped others would have been powerful reasons against their elevation in any representative democracy.
>
> ... It is difficult to see what other method than the nominating convention is available; more, it is true to say that, on balance, it has worked well rather than badly.
>
> ... It achieves the results that the needs of the people require.
>
> For there is at least one test of the system that is, I think, decisive. There have been five considerable crises in American history. There was the

need to start the republic adequately in 1789; it gave the American people its natural leader in George Washington. The crisis of 1800 brought
Jefferson to the presidency; that of 1861 brought Abraham Lincoln. The
War of 1914 found Woodrow Wilson in office; the great depression
resulted in the election of Franklin Roosevelt. So far, it is clear, the hour
has brought forth the man.[7]

(The administration of Franklin Roosevelt was a time for writing favorably of presidents and the way they were chosen.)

The Election of a President

Once a presidential candidate is named, party members normally
put differences aside and work for his election. Whatever their personal preferences, they are willing not to press the candidate to declare
himself on questions of policy in the hope that a contrived ambiguity
in campaign statements will result in a broader appeal to the electorate, a victory in November, and the rewards of office. They contribute
money and time to permit professionals in public relations to peddle an
"image" of the candidate to the electorate.

The accepted rule in American campaigning is that an unequivocal
statement of policy loses more votes than it gains. A politician who
wishes to win either remains silent—the favored strategy of popular
incumbents seeking reelection—or he equivocates. In any event he
avoids alienating people on policy matters and, more subtly, leaves
them room to fill in the spaces with wish-fulfilling fantasies. The public
has a talent for clothing a candidate with its own ideals. Although
Hubert Humphrey and Richard Nixon carefully hewed to the line
down the middle of the road during the 1968 campaign, advocating
neither escalation nor prompt withdrawal from Vietnam, there was a
strong tendency of dovish Democrats and dovish Republicans alike to
see the candidates of their respective parties as dovish, and of hawks to
see their men as hawkish.[8] A Republican favoring a tougher war policy,
for example, was likely to see Nixon as a hawk—and in addition to see
Humphrey as a dove. Even if the candidate of one's party takes a firm
stand, there is a tendency of the average voter to misperceive it and
substitute his own view, if it differs from the candidate's, or to forget
it entirely.[9] But fantasy flows more freely if the candidate remains
uncommitted.

Some candidates break the rule, of course, but few who do win general elections. In 1964 Barry Goldwater made clear policy statements,
some deliberately and some shooting from the hip. His politically suici-

dal declarations in support of escalation in Vietnam and in opposition to civil rights, social security, and the Tennessee Valley Authority were made against the advice of pragmatists within the party. In 1968 George Wallace alone among the three leading candidates spoke explicitly on policy, but he was appealing to a fairly homogeneous portion of the electorate rather than to a broad coalition. In 1972 Richard Nixon said less—and when he did speak, less of substance—than any presidential candidate in living memory, while Senator McGovern hurt his candidacy by issuing substantive policy statements on domestic and foreign issues. George McGovern shared Barry Goldwater's I'd-rather-be-right-than-president heresy. Both lost by wide margins.

The candidate's main contribution to the exchange up to election day is to build a winning coalition, a simple plurality of voters in the general election. His strategic problem is to appeal to a good number of geographic, racial, ethnic, class, age, and other groups without alienating too many others. But it is difficult to appeal for support without violating the campaign rule against policy commitments. Only on an issue of proven popularity, which will alienate at most a small, expendable minority, can the candidate afford to be definite. Richard Nixon's explicit opposition to the busing of school children for purposes of racial integration is a case in point. Public opinion polls showed an overwhelming majority of Americans in the late 1960s and the 1970s to be strongly against busing. But commitments without costs at all are possible too. They may be advanced in private to key people inside and outside of the government. Or they may be made in ways that have few policy implications or none at all, such as a promise of appointment of a member of a given group to the cabinet, the Supreme Court, or a lesser post, or a candidate's well-publicized visit to an interest group convention or an ethnic group outing.

Normally a convention responds to a presidential candidate's wishes with respect to a vice-presidential candidate and a platform; both are coalition-building devices. The candidate for vice-president is chosen to balance the ticket. If the presidential candidate is a liberal Catholic from the East, the second man should be, let us say, a conservative Protestant from the South or West. The platform performs the same function. Representatives of party factions and interest groups make proposals for inclusion in the platform, which is approved by the full convention. The likelihood of repercussions from groups which might disagree with these proposals in a direct confrontation is not great, because the platform is not meant to be acted upon or even remembered long after the delegates go home. There are exceptions. In 1964 Barry Goldwater dominated the writing of the platform at the Republican convention with the intention of demonstrating that he and his supporters controlled the party. He openly beat down suggestions inconsistent with his program and made the platform a symbol of the exclusiveness rather than the inclusiveness of the party. Senator Goldwater's choice of a fellow conservative as a running mate, though he came from another part of the country, was equally unconventional.

In composing a platform, a ticket, or a cabinet, the candidate for president must decide how much to reward friends and assure their continued support and how much to reach out to invite the support of others and enlarge his electoral and postelection coalition. As in traditional economic problems with apples and oranges, solutions depend upon the value each participant attaches to each commodity, a value which tends to diminish as the number of its kind one possesses increases. In most cases a mixture is valued the most. In coalition-building through cabinet nominations, for example, it may pay to honor a few important groups outside the candidate's core of supporters, but at some point there will be less profit in the nomination of another interest representative than in that of a friend or associate to reassure the candidate's loyal supporters and to contribute to cabinet cohesiveness and morale.

In forming his election coalition—openly or covertly, with policy commitments or without—the candidate for president needs a general plan for maximizing votes and a specific plan for exploiting the idiosyncrasies of the electoral college.

Once every thirty or forty years, a new electoral coalition is formed in the United States, giving one of the major parties the advantage in presidential elections until the next realignment. In 1896, the Republicans consolidated an electoral coalition of manufacturing interests and industrial labor, a lasting majority cutting across class lines.[10] In 1932 and other elections of the period, the Democrats created a new coalition along class lines: the underprivileged, the South, a few patricians such as Franklin Roosevelt himself, and the intellectuals.[11] In intervening years the White House may be captured by another party, but typically without maintaining control of Congress. Wilson lost his Democratic majorities in both houses of Congress in 1919; the Republicans lost their control of Congress in 1955, only halfway into the first of Dwight Eisenhower's two terms; and Richard Nixon *began* his administration with a majority of Democrats in Congress, which suggests that the Democratic coalition of 1932 still had life.[12] The general strategy is to compose a coalition that can live together, even if uneasily, as long as the coalitions of 1896 and 1932 did.

The biases of the electoral college as it works now are not the biases intended by the framers of the Constitution. Accordingly, party strategists adapt to present realities. As originally planned, the electoral college was meant to have been a nominating body in most years, leaving the final choice to the House of Representatives when there was no majority. But under the impact of a two-party system and state laws prescribing a winner-take-all popular vote for electoral slates within each state, it has come to be an electing body, quite by accident favoring large two-party states. The preferred strategy has been to try for an electoral college victory by appealing to uncommitted voters in enough large states to win a majority of electors. In practice this strategy has inflated the influence of ethnic and racial minorities in the cities in the selection of the president, balancing in some measure the disproportionate influence of rural voters over the legislative branch. This system therefore encourages a candidate to favor certain groups of voters over others as he constructs his electoral coalition.

Understandably, groups not favored by the operation of the electoral college have called for its reform or abolition. And nearly everyone is concerned that it may elect a candidate who has lost the popular vote, as it did in 1888. Unfortunately the same mishap could occur under the terms of the two most popular reforms: both the district plan and the proportional plan would have resulted in the election of Richard Nixon over John Kennedy in 1960.[13] Direct election seemed the logical alternative for critics of the present system, since it would put an end to special benefits for urban minorities, eliminate worries about electing the wrong man, and have a straightforward appeal to believers in democratic processes. A constitutional amendment was imminent. But then George Wallace demonstrated in 1968 that the electoral college might favor rural rather than urban voters. With a little more luck than he had, a regional third-party candidate could prevent either of the two main parties' candidates from winning the required majority of electors, and could then bargain for concessions or a coalition with one of them as the price of support in the college or the House of Representatives. Because of this situation, the South abruptly lost interest in reform, and the amendment died.

When candidates and segments of the party maneuver for advantage within the existing electoral system or take sides in the debate on electoral reform, they are engaged in the normal party business of building coalitions as efficiently as they can in order to win elections.

The Disruption of Normal Exchange

In the close exchange associated with successful campaigning for office, the candidate works to construct an electoral coalition and promises rewards for his supporters if he wins. Members of the party contribute their time, money, and votes, and both sides avoid behavior that might drive voters away. But sometimes the concern over winning office leads to a falling out between the president or the candidate and his party, if one side concludes that it will not profit from an impending electoral exchange.

Party members may withdraw support from a presidential candidate who seems unlikely to reward them with patronage or appropriate policy leadership if he is elected. In 1964 many Republicans viewed the candidacy of Barry Goldwater as a capturing of the party by radicals with whom they would be unable to do business after the election; in 1972 many Democrats had similar feelings about Senator McGovern's candidacy. Each candidate was regarded as a man of conscience rather than a willing participant in traditional political exchange—inner-directed rather than other-directed[14]—and therefore a threat. For moderates and traditionalists within the party, the rational strategy was to sit on their hands, as the saying goes, perhaps to do some circumspect sabotage during the campaign, and to vote secretly for the opponent in November. Control of the party was wrested from each candidate shortly after his defeat, and the status quo was restored.

Comparably, members of the party may wish to deny renomination to a president, however faithful a bargainer, who appears likely to lose his next election. "Dumping" a president is difficult, though, because of the patronage and publicity the incumbent commands.

Harry Truman faced opposition from party leaders when the time came for his nomination as candidate for the presidency in 1948. A second-rank political figure until the moment he succeeded to the presidency upon the death of Franklin Roosevelt in 1945, Harry Truman had endured three stormy years in office, lost control of Congress to the Republicans in mid-term elections in 1946, engineered the passage of the Marshall Plan, suffered the passage of the Taft-Hartley Act over his veto in 1947, and at last dropped so far in public esteem that an earnest search was undertaken for a replacement in the 1948 campaign. A broad coalition of liberal and conservative Democratic leaders ranging from Hubert Humphrey to Strom Thurmond asked General Eisenhower late in the spring of 1948 to be their new candidate. He declined. There was little doubt that he could have had the nomination for the asking, and an easy election afterwards. Justice William O. Douglas was approached a while later and also declined. The convention which nominated Harry Truman in 1948 did so without enthusiasm, confident of his defeat in November.

After his unexpected victory and another term in the White House, President Truman again seemed more a liability than an asset to the party as election time approached. He was held responsible for an unpopular war in Korea and for allowing subversion and corruption in the federal government. In the New Hampshire primary early in March, Estes Kefauver, who had won a reputation as a crime-fighter on the strength of some televised hearings in the Senate, beat Truman by a comfortable margin. Before the month was out, the President announced his decision not to run again, to the satisfaction of many members of his party. By this time General Eisenhower had stated his willingness to be the Republican candidate, and Democrats began the hopeless task of finding someone to compete in November.

In 1968, during another unpopular Asian war, Democrats forced another president to withdraw. Criticism of Lyndon Johnson's conduct of the war in Vietnam culminated in the surprising showing of his archcritic, Eugene McCarthy, in the New Hampshire primary. Once again before the end of March a president announced his decision to retire from office. Although both men insisted otherwise, it is not unreasonable to think that they would have sought reelection if the party had encouraged them.

When an incumbent seems likely to win if renominated, no serious opposition to his candidacy develops. Whatever the dissatisfactions with President Eisenhower among Republican professionals in 1956,[15] there was no opposition to his renomination. He was more popular than ever in the country, and that was what mattered. In 1971 and 1972 ideological opposition to the renomination of Richard Nixon, from the left (in the campaign of antiwar congressman Paul McCloskey) and from the right (in the movement of the Young Americans for Freedom to nominate the vice-president for the presidency), captured some headlines but proved lifeless in the primaries and the convention, where it would have counted. President Nixon was conceded to have the best chance of any Republican in the 1972 election and the party rallied behind him. The denial of renomination, when it does occur, is a calculated jettisoning of dead weight without ideological complications.

When increasingly embarrassing questions about White House involvement in the Watergate affair surfaced in Senate hearings during President Nixon's second term, some Republicans in the Senate and House of Representatives issued public declarations of their independence of the president as party leader and, retrospectively, of his conduct of the 1972 campaign. There was no intention of dropping the president, who was at that point ineligible for reelection, but the frame of mind resembled that of the Democrats who had turned against Harry Truman or Lyndon Johnson in election year: they had come to regard the leader of their party as an electoral liability.

A president, too, will avoid exchanges when he anticipates a bad bargain. There are several variations in which the president adjusts his coalition by excluding some, reaches to include some not in the party at the time, or does both simultaneously. Some of the adjustments are mild, some major.

Two of the most ruthless and successful presidents severed their ties with party machines early in their careers as they were working their way up to the White House. Each had entered state politics with the help of Democratic bosses and repudiated them shortly afterwards. Woodrow Wilson was a machine candidate for governor of New Jersey in 1910. He owed his nomination to party bosses who considered a university president an attractive candidate in a year of popular reaction against old-line politicians. He was a candidate who stood a good chance of pulling a Democratic legislature into office on his coattails, they thought, who would be no threat to the continuance of the machine behind the scenes. One of the party leaders was particularly interested in being chosen United States Senator by the new state legislature, as it was done in those days. Wilson's public repudiation of the bosses of his party during the campaign helped him amass a comfortable margin of votes in the general election.[16] Franklin Roosevelt became a state senator in New York the same year, as the choice of party bosses, and turned upon the regular organization, including the leaders of Tammany Hall, as soon as he was sworn into office. He gained national prominence in the state legislature by opposing the machine's candidate for United States Senator and later went to Washington to work under Wilson and share in his alliance with the forces of progressivism.[17]

Lyndon Johnson bypassed elements of his party when it suited him, a practice that contributed to his vulnerability when pressures to remove him mounted within the party in 1968. He, like a number of recent chief executives, used the President's Club to raise funds for the national organization, for example, rewarding donors of a thousand dollars or more with White House dinners, meetings with high officials of the executive branch, color photographs of the president, and, according to Republican critics, with favored treatment before administrative tribunals. State Democratic organizations complained that the President's Club drained support from state and local campaigns by tapping their largest contributors directly. And like many presidents, Johnson also preferred a nonpartisan stance in his dealings with the public and Congress. As a senator from a one-party state, a Senate leader under a Republican president, a presidential candidate wooing moderate Republican voters from Barry Goldwater, and a president striving for national consensus, Lyndon Johnson consistently strove to broaden his coalition across party lines.

The most serious avoidance of exchange with the party, more often contemplated than carried out, is an attempt to establish a new party by realigning the coalition to exclude refractory elements of the old party and to attract new components in the hope of building a more viable organization. Abraham Lincoln took a long step in that direction in the election of 1864 when he accepted the nomination of the Union party of Republicans and War Democrats and ran with a Democrat, Andrew Johnson, as his vice-presidential candidate. With both parties divided over the Civil War and with movements inside the Republican party before and after the nominating convention seeking a replacement for President Lincoln, it made good sense to seek a realignment. In 1912 Theodore Roosevelt formed a new party to run against the Republicans' candidate when he was refused their nomination. Neither Roosevelt nor the Republican candidate won. Establishing a new party is a bold move—and a grave threat to the regular organization.

Both Franklin Roosevelt and Dwight Eisenhower gave some thought to realignment during times of trouble with the conservative wings of their parties. Roosevelt longed for the support of liberals and progressives within the Republican fold, particularly when members of his own party in Congress turned against him in the late 1930s, but his dreams of a new liberal Democratic party did not materialize because he was unwilling to take the risks of a sustained campaign against the southern conservatives and northern city bosses whose departure might have made way for a new coalition. Dwight Eisenhower grew increasingly disenchanted with the Republican party as his administration wore on, to the point of questioning whether the party deserved to live. He could not understand the unfriendliness of congressional Republicans or their unwillingness to assume international responsibilities.[18]

Whether initiated by the president or his party, a disruption of customary transactions can usually be traced to a pragmatic determination that greater profits lie elsewhere.

Abnormally Intense Exchanges

Presidents and presidential candidates sometimes engage in intense interactions with members of the party, forming strong ideological or personal bonds that transcend the usual businesslike exchange of votes, jobs, legislation, and other tangibles. The psychic rewards of an intimate exchange may contribute to defeat in the election by drawing attention from the requirements of coalition-building. A rational politician whose immediate goal is election resists the temptation to be close to a limited number of party members, therefore, and distributes his campaign resources broadly enough to have the best chance of winning office. In the same manner, a president who concentrates his bargaining resources too narrowly risks the loss of the support he needs for his legislative program in Congress.

The political career of Woodrow Wilson illustrates both the rational and the irrational uses of party. He was among the most effective of party leaders and, at times, among the least successful. As a young man enamored of the British political system he proposed that the government of the United States, which he considered the captive of special interests, be reformed by turning over the power of the committees of Congress to a responsible set of party leaders who would be, at once, the cabinet and the managers of the business of the legislature. By the time he ran for governor of New Jersey, however, Wilson had come to the conclusion that executive leadership through a strong party organization was a more practicable way than constitutional reform to bring about effective democratic government. He conceived of the governor and the president as tribunes of the people, the most broadly representative and therefore the most authoritative figures in their governments, who could draw forces together within the existing system of formally separated powers. His election as governor, his election and reelection to the White House, the respect he enjoyed in the country, and his notable success as a leader of legislatures are testament to his abilities as a partisan politician.

But he went too far. In his reelection campaign in 1916, Wilson incautiously allowed his party to use the theme "He kept us out of war!" and to paint the opposition as the party of war: "If You want WAR, vote for HUGHES! If You want Peace with Honor, VOTE FOR WILSON!"[19] The candidate himself said, "If you elect my opponent you elect a war."[20] Six months later he had been forced into war. In the mid-term campaign of 1918 Wilson appealed to the voters for a Democratic victory, only to have Republicans take control of both houses of Congress. After the war his excessive partisanship in refusing the Republican party more than token representation in the peace negotiations was one reason for the rejection of the peace treaty by the Senate. The partisanship that carried him to a position of world leadership grew narrow and hastened his downfall at the end of his term of office.

A more common deviation from the norm of businesslike exchange is that of the unsuccessful presidential candidate who cannot transcend the role of factional leader when the time comes to appeal to other factions of his party. George McGovern, the Democratic candidate in 1972, is an example. His relations with the liberal-to-left wing of the party were ideologically and personally close. The candidate was unusually explicit about policy; his followers were loyal, more generous with contributions than the supporters of centrists, and tireless.

Although his campaign was doomed from the outset, in all probability, Senator McGovern made every effort to broaden his appeal the moment his nomination was assured. In the convention he resisted the inclusion in the platform of radical demands made by some of his own supporters. He chose a running mate who would balance the ticket in the traditional manner, and did so again when his first vice-presidential candidate withdrew. And during the campaign he courted the votes of groups that he was, according to public opinion polls, losing to Richard Nixon. He failed. A principled faction of the party had nominated a man whose appeal was unalterably narrow. His attempts to broaden his policy and adjust his image were unavailing.

The candidacy of McGovern differed in one respect from the bids of Barry Goldwater for the presidency and Eugene McCarthy for the nomination in the years before: McGovern tried doggedly to move to the center during the campaign. Goldwater's continuing interaction with ideologists of the right, certain to alienate others, seemed consciously self-destructive. But then, neither he nor his running mate appeared to care a great deal about winning. McCarthy too was casual about strategy and uncompromising in matters of policy. He and Goldwater were sheltered by devoted followers from the realities of vote-bargaining in American politics.

Senator McGovern would not have been nominated in 1972 if he and other Democrats had not made changes in the process of selecting delegates that gave new groups—including many of his supporters—access to the convention. From the Democrats' unhappy convention and defeat at the polls in 1968 had come pressure for reform. In 1969 the national chairman of the party named George McGovern to head a commission to make findings and recommendations. The commission determined that many of the delegates to the 1968 convention had been selected long before the campaign had begun. In some states they found few or no rules governing delegate selection, and in numerous cases the selection proved to be rigged against insurgents, as in the holding of selection meetings before the appointed hour. And even where the naming of delegates went according to rule, the winner-take-all tradition discouraged minority representation. The result was a convention of older people, typically large contributors to the party, said McGovern, who gave the nomination to a man whose stand-ins had done badly in the primaries. The guidelines formulated by the commission, many of which were adopted by the party in time for the 1972 convention, included an end to discriminatory assessments of delegates, an end to discrimination by age and sex, a guarantee of participation by minority members, and an open selection process starting late enough in the year to allow the members some knowledge of the array of candidates and issues their choices would affect.[21]

Unfortunately for the Democratic party, an influx of amateurs of every description in 1972 did not assure a convention attuned to public demands, any more than a traditional convention with gross overrepresentation of older, wealthier, more highly educated white males assured the nomination of an unpopular candidate. After the election the party selected new leaders and retreated from the McGovern reforms.

There had been movements to reform the Democratic and Republican parties before, to transform them from limited-purpose, limited-participation, seasonal organizations into something at once more popular and more effective. Woodrow Wilson, borrowing from the British, was the intellectual patron of the reform movement in this century. His thinking was reflected in a report of the Committee on Political Parties of the American Political Science Association in 1950, "Toward a More Responsible Two-Party System." This report proposed a more active, policy-minded, cohesive kind of organization for the major parties. Under the terms of the proposal each party would hold a national convention every two years to reformulate its national legislative program, and would hold state conventions soon after to draft state legislative proposals consistent with the national platform. A strengthened national committee, assisted by a party council, would speak for the party between conventions. In Congress, leadership was to be centralized and tightened to induce legislators of each party to vote together in a disciplined manner to enact the platform policies.[22] The Committee on Political Parties envisioned a kind of party that would revitalize the system of government in the United States by increasing the interest and participation of the members, encouraging them to deal with issues, and tying the rank and file to their elected officials.

Some minor reforms in this direction took place in the Democratic party in the 1950s under the influence of presidential candidate Adlai Stevenson. In parts of New York and California and a number of other places, issue-conscious men and women who had been repelled by the business-like, lower-middle-class nature of many local Democratic party organizations, were recruited into middle- and upper-middle-class "clubs" and in some instances displaced the traditional organizations. Nationally a Democratic Advisory Council was formed to give the party leadership in a time when the Republicans controlled the White House. All major segments of the party were to be represented. But congressional leaders, jealous of their independence, boycotted the council. Neither reform had a lasting effect.

Thorough Wilsonian responsible-party reform is unlikely in the United States. It would require more rank-and-file participation, the abolition of the direct primary, probably, centralization and discipline in the direction of party organizations, a new concern about policy, and a willingness to be ideologically distinctive—to provide "a choice, not an echo." But people in the United States do not favor these changes. Among most of the better educated, in particular, there seems to be support for the existing party system and rejection of the ideas of party discipline and ideological homogeneity.[23] Furthermore, Wilson himself demonstrated, at least for a time, that a president can be a strong partisan leader in a weak party system. Successful presidents have reveled in party politics and made the best of scarce resources.

Conclusion

American party members, presidential candidates, and presidents are ready to do business with one another, with election and reelection as the prime goal upon which others of varying importance depend. The exchange tends to be quite straightforward: electoral support by members of the party in return for the promise of leadership in public policy, campaign assistance for lesser candidates, and patronage. For his part the presidential candidate, and the president if he runs again, must work to build a winning coalition.

At times old networks of exchange are disrupted when a president reconstructs his coalition with an eye to the next election or perhaps to improved public and congressional relations in the interim, or when the party drops an incumbent for a more popular leader. Such disruptions are infrequent and in that sense abnormal, but they do not represent a departure from the businesslike frame of mind which compels each side above all to improve its chances of winning the next election. On the contrary, they illustrate this single-mindedness in its purest and most ruthless state.

At other times, however, an intense relationship develops between a party faction and a party leader—who may become the candidate for president—that subordinates victory at the polls to other values. The result is defeat at the nominating or electing stage, reassertion of control by the old guard, and a restoration of traditional values. Intense commitment to a set of persons or ideas is not the mark of a normal, successful actor in the American political system. Spreading resources thin to attract a winning coalition is both the rational strategy and the psychic bent of the typical politician.

Notes

[1]Patrick Anderson, *The Presidents' Men* (Garden City, N.Y.: Doubleday & Company, Inc., 1969), p. 181. See Anthony Downs, *An Economic Theory of Democracy* (New York: Harper & Row, Publishers, 1957), pp. 28–30 on the motivation of party activity.

[2]Lewis Chester *et al., An American Melodrama: The Presidential Campaign of 1968* (New York: The Viking Press, Inc., 1969), pp. 185, 219, 253–54.

[3]Austin Ranney, "Turnout and Representation in Presidential Primary Elections," *American Political Science Review,* LXVI, No. 1 (1972), 21–37.

[4]Philip E. Converse *et al.,* "Continuity and Change in American Politics," *American Political Science Review,* LXIII, No. 4 (1969), 1092–93.

[5]*New York Times,* February 21, 1920, p. 3.

[6]James Bryce, *The American Commonwealth* (2d ed. rev.) (New York: The Macmillan Company, 1891), I, 73–75.

[7]Harold J. Laski, *The American Presidency* (New York: Harper & Brothers Publishers, 1940), pp. 49–52.

[8]Benjamin I. Page and Richard A. Brody, "Policy Voting and the Electoral Process: The Vietnam War Issue," *American Political Science Review,* LXVII, No. 3 (1972), 987; Downs, *Economic Theory of Democracy,* Chap. 8, particularly p. 136 on "trying to be as ambiguous as possible."

[9]Bernard R. Berelson *et al., Voting* (Chicago: University of Chicago Press, 1954), pp. 215–33.

[10]V. O. Key, *Politics, Parties, and Pressure Groups* (4th ed.) (New York: Thomas Y. Crowell Company, 1958), pp. 188–89.

[11]Angus Campbell et al., *The American Voter* (New York: John Wiley & Sons, Inc., 1960), pp. 531–38.

[12]But see Kevin Phillips, *The Emerging Republican Majority* (New York: Arlington House, Inc., 1969).

[13]Senate Committee on the Judiciary, Subcommittee on Constitutional Amendments, *Election of the President,* 89th Cong., 2d sess., and 90th Cong., 1st sess., 1966–1967, pp. 233–34.

[14]David Riesman, *The Lonely Crowd* (New Haven: Yale University Press, 1950), Chap. 1.

[15]Richard E. Neustadt, *Presidential Power* (New York: The New American Library Inc., 1964), Chap. 4.

[16]James M. Burns, *The Deadlock of Democracy* (1st rev. ed.) (Englewood Cliffs, N.J.: Prentice-Hall, Inc., 1963), pp. 123–27.

[17]Rexford G. Tugwell, *The Democratic Roosevelt* (Baltimore: Penguin Books Inc., 1969), pp. 68–77.

[18]Burns, *Deadlock of Democracy,* pp. 167–73, 193–94.

[19]Arthur S. Link and William M. Leary, Jr., "Election of 1916," in *The Coming to Power,* ed. Arthur M. Schlesinger, Jr. (New York: Chelsea House Publishers, 1971), p. 318.

[20]Richard P. Longaker, "Woodrow Wilson and the Presidency," in *The Philosophy and Policies of Woodrow Wilson,* ed. Earl Latham (Chicago: University of Chicago Press, 1958), p. 79, 44 n.

[21]George McGovern, "The Lessons of 1968," *Harpers,* September, 1970, pp. 43–47.

[22]*American Political Science Review,* XLIV, No. 3 (1950), Supplement, 5–14.

[23]Jack Dennis, "Support for the Party System by the Mass Public," *American Political Science Review,* LX, No. 3 (1966), 606.

t
w
o
The President and His Advisors

Presidents long for good advice. Strong national leaders who want the ingredients of decision within reach for plotting changes in the course of government share this necessity with passive presidents who prefer perfected advice and relief from the burden of decision. Presidents all look for able advisors, wistfully it seems—witness the ritual vow to attract "the best minds" to Washington as the term begins—and in the end settle, perhaps, for less.[1]

The difficulty is that advisors of the stature and variety a president needs are hard to find or to retain on his terms. Many a president has been exasperated about the quality of advice in the White House. Even if they can be discovered, the best minds cannot be induced to serve when the costs of giving advice loom too large. If the full costs are learned only after work has begun, advisors may offer less advice or leave. The president who understands the needs of advisors and exploits the rewards and pains of office will come closest to securing the advice he wants.

The president-advisor relationship rests on an expectation of mutual gain. Each party reckons that an exchange will bring benefits outweighing costs by a margin wider than alternative exchanges afford. In the history of these exchanges, regularities appear in the benefits and costs to the president and to his advisors.

Leaving aside honesty and intelligence, which are difficult to measure in a public figure, two traits seem most to affect an advisor's usefulness to the president: length of service, which is related to loyalty, and involvement in interests outside the White House. Expressing each as a continuum, we have a two-dimensional field for the analysis of advisors. Each trait is linked with a peculiar kind of advice needed by the president. Loyal, long-term associates lend support and counsel discreetly in moments of pressure and crisis. Those who are independent of the president, particularly experts from corporations and the

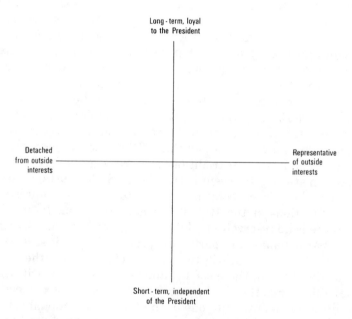

professions invited for brief service, are a source of fresh ideas. One who is detached from outside interests can put himself in the president's position and offer disinterested analysis and opinion. And one who represents outside interests through his affiliation with an economic, racial, or other segment of society can give the president realistic policy suggestions and political intelligence. At one time or another a president needs advisors with each of these qualities.

From the point of view of the advisors, the rewards of working for the White House include public service, career advancement, fame, and power. The exchange between president and advisor occurs and persists only as long as each side stands to gain. The parties to the transaction weigh costs too. Advisors run the risk of being ignored, suffering public or private abuse, or abrupt removal at the whim of the president. Not infrequently they accept cuts in salary in moving from private employment to government service. The president's risks are every bit as serious, and as a result he and his advisors or prospective advisors are often at odds. A president must struggle to attract and keep the best people because the costs are high for them, and he may drive advisors away because the costs are too high for him. The risks are so high on both sides, in fact, that only the momentousness of the mutual rewards makes the transaction possible at all.

A president needs a balance of all four kinds of advice in order to avoid the diminishing marginal returns of one-sided intelligence. And he must watch for signs that advice has turned sour. Loyalty may become sycophancy. The new ideas of an independent advisor may prove irrelevant or fatally abstract. The representation of outside interests may give veto groups such power that government stagnates or become so crass as to disrupt morale and community of purpose in the White House. And too-perfect detachment from those interests insulates an advisor from the realities of his political environment.

In Great Britain the cabinet is a great pool of talent, and by tradition its members are freer than their American counterparts to play more than one role at a time, notably that of factional representative and loyal, discreet advisor. The traditions of secrecy and collective responsibility, which are largely absent in the United States, sustain those roles even when there is no personal loyalty to the prime minister. The advisory functions of the British cabinet are broad. In the United States there is no reservoir of advisors comparable to the British cabinet and the parliamentary party, less prestige in public service generally, and far fewer institutional expectations in the advisory relationship. Without these constraints an advisor may drift from his original role, for better or for worse, either to adapt to new White House needs or to lapse into one of the four dysfunctional roles. And so it is that presidents hire experimentally, tentatively to fill special needs. It is a rare advisor to the president who is versatile enough to excel in several roles. Modern examples are Harry Hopkins, relief administrator, cabinet member, special ambassador, confidant, and handyman for Franklin Roosevelt, and Clark Clifford, at various times White House staff member, senior consultant, and cabinet member for Presidents Truman, Kennedy, and Johnson, who exhibited qualities of loyalty, intelligence, tact, worldliness, selflessness, and independence of mind, a remarkable concentration of talent in one man.

The usual pattern, from which Hopkins and Clifford departed, is a rough division of labor among several kinds of advisors. Presidents differ in the mix of advisors they attract. Harry Truman relied more heavily than most on his cabinet and his cronies, Dwight Eisenhower more on the White House staff. Richard Nixon shied away from the advice of all but a few people. At the other extreme, Franklin Roosevelt gathered information and ideas from a profusion of sources inside and outside of government. He was at home in the presence of people of all stations and persuasions and unintimidated by unorthodoxy, brilliance, or strength of character in an advisor. As a result he was temperamentally more fit than many chief executives to fashion and exploit a complex advisory system with such dissimilar people as his trusted, long-time secretary, assistant, and hostess, "Missy" LeHand; intractable cabinet member Jesse Jones, barely tolerated for long years because of his ties with Congress and the business community; and the outspoken plant geneticist, ascetic, and mystic, Henry Wallace.

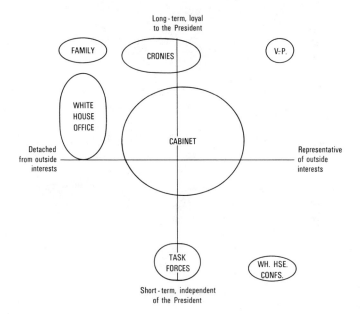

Franklin Roosevelt had the advantage of time in building his advisory system; several of his closest advisors had been with him for many years before he won the presidency. Only Kennedy of the recent presidents had the same head start. By comparison, Harry Truman and Dwight Eisenhower reached the White House virtually unattended and in crucial respects unprepared, and suffered for it.

In this chapter we shall examine the normal level of exchange between the president and the cabinet, the White House Office, members of the family, cronies, task forces, and White House conferences, and also some deviant relationships in which the president is unusually close to or distant from his advisors.

The President's Cabinet

The cabinet is a diverse group, typically, and functionally diffuse, although not to the extent that the British cabinet is. The American version consists of older, established men and an occasional woman who are useful to a president, both practically and symbolically, because of their expertise and outside affiliations. They are not his most intimate advisors, normally, or even notably loyal to him.[2]

The American cabinet, as a body, usually does not make decisions or advise on questions of importance, although individually its members often do both. In these respects its development has diverged from the British cabinet, which evolved from an advisory to a decision-making body in which binding votes are taken. Some early presidents of the

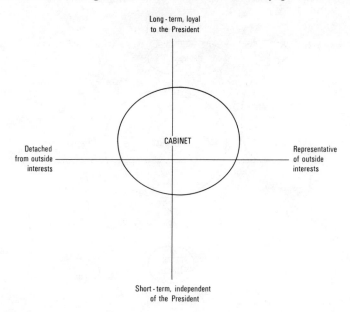

United States experimented with voting, but the practice was abandoned. George Washington led off by consulting his department heads as a group, and before long the term "cabinet" came into use. (Until the ratification of the Twenty-fifth Amendment on presidential disability in 1967, the cabinet had no collective function under the Constitution, and has never had a constitutional mandate to decide or advise collectively on other matters. It is not described as a cabinet, in fact, but as the "principal officers" of the "executive departments" in Article II of the Constitution and the Twenty-fifth Amendment.) Both Washington and Jefferson went so far as to abide by votes in cabinet meetings. In the administrations of William Henry Harrison and James

Buchanan the cabinet ran the government briefly, but the relationship that won out is epitomized in a remark in cabinet credited to President Lincoln: "Seven noes, one aye—the ayes have it."

With the addition of cabinet-level departments on the order of agriculture, labor, and commerce, as much to represent the interests of groups in the society as to pursue general governmental functions, reliance on the cabinet for corporate policy-making became less plausible. In its political, administrative, and advisory functions a cabinet is what the president makes of it, but even under a Truman or an Eisenhower, who took theirs seriously, it does not approach the British in power and repute.

Individually, members of the cabinet may be or become well known, particularly if their interests and affiliations are prized by the president and the people. Men of reputation sought by a president for his cabinet can be a boon to him politically and administratively even if they are unsuitable members of an advisory or decision-making team. In enlisting Henry Stimson as secretary of war in 1940, Franklin Roosevelt brought to the government a senior Republican statesman, an important symbol of bipartisanship in the prosecution of the war and a man of rare experience as secretary of war under Taft and secretary of state under Hoover. It hardly mattered that he might differ with other members of the cabinet on issues beyond his jurisdiction.

A president need not even know his appointees to the cabinet if they come well recommended. Kennedy knew neither Dean Rusk nor Robert McNamara when he named them to the key cabinet posts of state and defense. McNamara was named because he was a captain of industry, a respected president of the Ford Motor Company. He was an independent Republican as well. Charles E. Wilson, a president of General Motors, was an equally remarkable secretary of defense under President Eisenhower.

The representation of business and other economic interests in the cabinet, the appointment of a member of the opposition party to curry bipartisan support in Congress, and deference to traditions of geographical and religious balance all tend to work against the development of a team spirit. A president cannot have it both ways—John Kennedy once tried, satisfying some of the demands of representativeness cheaply by arranging a symbolic offer of the postmaster generalship to black Congressman William Dawson of Chicago on the condition that he refuse it, which he did. Some, like Richard Nixon, preferred homogeneity and loyalty in their cabinets.

Excessive representation of non-White House interests in the cabinet is costly. Warren Harding's mixed cabinet of statesmen and scoundrels is an extreme example. It generated centrifugal pressures too great for a weak chief executive to control. In Eisenhower's cabinet the appointment of an active Democrat and head of the AFL plumber's union, Martin Durkin, as secretary of labor proved an embarrassment. Secretary Durkin lasted less than eight months in a businessman's administration, unable to keep the delicate balance of roles demanded by the president, who specified that Durkin "would be expected to represent labor's viewpoint in the government but ... he would no longer owe personal allegiance to labor, only to the nation." President Eisenhower's guideline for Durkin was a manager's dream: the secretary was to "voice his own convictions honestly and forthrightly" but to "accept and abide by my decisions, once made." According to the president, Durkin "seemed to have difficulty making this distinction, which to me was quite simple."[3] President Nixon's second-term secretary of labor, Peter Brennan, a union leader, had similar problems satisfying the White House and organized labor simultaneously. Even when they are selected for purposes other than interest representation, cabinet members tend to develop special interests, departmental or personal. A president who values teamwork tempts fate in giving antagonistic groups representation in his cabinet.

In the Nixon administration, as in most others, the most trusted cabinet members were to be found in State, Defense or its predecessors, Justice, and the Treasury—the oldest and generally the most important of the departments—to which one may now add the young Department of Health, Education, and Welfare, with its broad and controversial responsibilities. Favored appointees move easily from subcabinet and cabinet posts in one department in this group to another. There is a like interchange of personnel between these departments and the White House Office. In contrast, the Departments of Agriculture, Commerce, Housing and Urban Development, Interior, Labor, and Transportation, which have somewhat closer ties with specific segments of the economy, are more tense and formal in their relations with the White House.[4]

For the cabinet member the rewards of the job include power, the pleasures of participation in national affairs, the satisfaction of public service, and for some the promotion of specific interests.

The costs, too, are great. The possibility of being a figurehead may discourage a person accustomed to leadership on his own terms. There is some danger of public attack and the unpleasantness it may bring oneself and one's family. The disruption of one's career and social ties, the monotony of life in Washington, "a city of southern efficiency and northern charm" in Kennedy's words, and frequently a loss of income are discouraging prospects. Theodore Sorensen noted with distress that the city of Los Angeles had twenty-eight positions with salaries higher than that of any cabinet post in the Kennedy administration.[5] For all of these reasons, the president is unlikely to attract the best people to the cabinet.

Some presidents have made serious efforts to hold meaningful meetings with the cabinets they have pieced together; others have thought them a waste of time. Two patterns of cabinet conduct have recurred: the orderly and the disorderly. Neither is notably successful. Meetings of the Eisenhower cabinet were planned and decorous, opening with a prayer by one of the churchmen in the group and continuing with formal presentations scheduled and rehearsed well in advance, more for the edification of colleagues than for debate and criticism. The president would interrupt now and then with personal reflections, judgments, and inspirational talks. Jolted only by the enthusiastic outbursts of Secretary Wilson and stormy declamations from the president himself, the sessions were valued by the president mainly for the inculcation of a spirit of reconciliation and mutual endeavor.

Woodrow Wilson and Franklin Roosevelt, at the other extreme, allowed cabinet meetings of a very different sort, characterized by rambling, sometimes pointless, and frequently exasperating contributions by the assembled amateurs on all manner of subjects, with none of the planning, staff work, and deliberate lackluster of the orderly regime. Wilson's tended to wander from one subject to another, grand and trivial alike, with rumors and anecdotes interspersed. President Roosevelt's, as the record of a 1941 meeting indicates, could go unguided from draft rejects through the smuggling of jewelry, the quality of food in Britain, oil, and radio stations in Nevada, then on to labor problems.[6]

Neither style is of much use to the chief executive. Good advice is not the likely result of either meticulous planning or unfocused conversation. And to worsen matters, cabinet members themselves often have found the sessions aggravating. As Jesse Jones explained, "My principal reason for not having a great deal to say at cabinet meetings was that there was no one at the table who could be of help to me except the president, and when I needed to consult him, I did not choose a cabinet meeting to do so." The casual remarks of colleagues may be both unhelpful and unwelcome. Consider the icy appraisal of Secretary of the Interior Albert Fall given by Secretary of State Charles Evans Hughes, former justice of the Supreme Court, presidential candidate, and governor of New York: "He would discourse at length on foreign affairs, showing neither acumen, discretion, nor accurate knowledge. But he thought he was an authority. His flow of words without wisdom was very boring to me at least, and I think to others. I had little to do with him. . . ."[7] In the Kennedy cabinet one member entertained his colleagues on all domestic and international questions with advice drawn from his limited public experience as mayor of Cleveland.

Most presidents feel free to ignore their cabinets, collectively and individually. Franklin Roosevelt, who was uninhibited in his exploitation of associates, often turned his back on men whose value lay in representing and communicating with outside interests or in administrative talent rather than in wisdom or personal rapport. Thus Secretary of the Interior Harold Ickes might complain of not having seen his president for a year and Secretary of State Cordell Hull repeatedly suffer the indignity of learning that Roosevelt had dealt directly with subordinates in the department, trusting them for advice and action in preference to the secretary. Both men were useful, but their identification with interests outside the White House reduced their value as team members.

The White House Office

Presidents who want more intimate advice turn to the White House Office, the president's staff of assistants formalized by the Reorganization Act of 1939. Before 1939 presidents who needed close advisors paid them out of their own pocket or found them positions in departments and borrowed them back. To improve the management of men and information in the burgeoning executive branch, the Reorganization Act established an Executive Office of the President and at its center the White House Office, a select group whose accountability to the president alone was symbolized in their exemption from Senate confirmation.

The White House staff tend not to represent defined interests. They are detached, instead, and therefore well suited to think and act as the president's alter egos. They are unusually loyal to him, in many cases having served him in his progress through lesser political offices, and they tend to be younger than cabinet members.

These distinctions between the typical cabinet member and White House staffer do not hold in every case, to be sure. Some of the more interesting and uncomfortable advisors have been interest representatives in the White House and detached, loyal associates in the cabinet. More than most presidents, Richard Nixon valued loyalty in his cabinet, as in the appointment of a trusted associate, William Rogers, to head the State Department (although his experience was in domestic affairs) and other loyal friends John Mitchell and Robert Finch to head the departments of Justice and Health, Education, and Welfare. None of them was regarded as able in office. Finch was removed under severe crossfire to sanctuary in the White House where he would have been more at ease in the first place. Mitchell resigned and was later deeply implicated in the Watergate affair. Urban affairs expert Daniel Patrick Moynihan, on the other hand, was an interest representative, President Nixon's resident liberal Democratic intellectual, a lonely and implausible affirmation of the president's interest in cities and the concerns of intellectuals. Moynihan had the misfortune to attract barbs from all sides. His constituencies turned on him one by one, questioning both his ideas and his motives, and colleagues in government made his blunt memoranda to the president public, to the embarrassment of president and advisor alike. After a time Moynihan returned to Harvard. He might have lasted a few months longer in Franklin Roosevelt's administration. Another early member of Nixon's

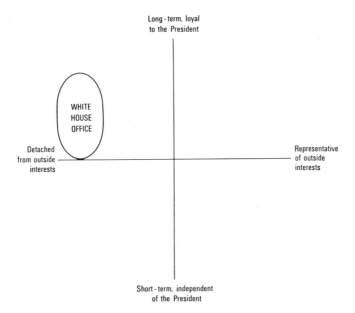

White House Office who had to leave, in this case for the Federal Reserve Board, was economist Arthur F. Burns. Moynihan and Burns were described, by way of epitaph, as believers among the nonbelievers of the White House.

The costs and benefits a president and a White House advisor must weigh to undertake their exchange and to maintain it are unique in the presidential advisory system. There are high risks and great rewards for both sides.

To the president, a good White House staff member is first of all detached from outside interests, including those of any department of government, and capable of taking a presidential perspective. Harry Hopkins had this ability in his role as adviser to Roosevelt, although he had other abilities and roles which make his classification difficult. A less complex example would be Richard Nixon's principal assistant for domestic affairs, John Ehrlichman, who replaced the Moynihan-Burns duo and offered the president a selflessness and tractability which they could not. "My knowledge of the kind of things we're dealing in here is very limited, and I'm the first to realize that," he said. "Sometimes it helps to be uneducated, so you can ask stupid questions . . . like 'Do we have to do this at all?' and 'Why can't the states do this?' "[8]

Detachment becomes a cost to the president when the advisor insulates himself from ideas other than those of the president and serves as a mirror rather than an informant. Naiveté of this kind is endemic in the White House. It is serious when there is a monopoly of such advisors, but presidents bring it upon themselves by appointing men of one kind for reasons of convenience and comfort—Lyndon Johnson's country boys or Richard Nixon's bland but ruthless lawyers and media men are examples.

Both Johnson and Nixon were criticized for allowing themselves to be isolated by their staffs. In 1970 the publication of a popular book on the subject by a disaffected former assistant to President Johnson, depicting the modern chief executive as a proud monarch and his staff as petty courtiers, coincided with a gnawing concern that President Nixon had lost touch with young people, dissenters, the under-privileged, and, most important, members of his own cabinet.[9] The White House took steps to reassure the country that the complaints were unfounded by reporting the exact number of people with whom the president was meeting regularly in his cabinet, the National Security Council, the economic advisory apparatus, and the White House staff. The secretary of state, with more devotion than accuracy, announced that he knew of no one "with an important problem" who could not see Mr. Nixon; but the concern hung on.[10] When the Watergate scandals surfaced later on, the peril of a persident's loss of contact with all but a few trusted advisors became clear.

Insulation of the president is most likely when his advice is channeled through one man, as in the case of Eisenhower's Sherman Adams in domestic matters and Nixon's Henry Kissinger in national security affairs. Each became nearly indispensable to the president, contrary to traditional warnings about monopolies in the White House. Adams alone decided who and what would reach the president's office. Eisenhower grew so dependent upon this one man that it took painfully long to remove him when Adams was found guilty of the kind of indiscretion that calls for instant dismissal. "I need him," said the president. Adams' power in the White House Office has known no equal, but then it is also true that domestic policy-making lapsed in the Eisenhower years, and on balance a less magisterial Hopkins, Sorensen, or Moyers may have held more real power.

The other value a president seeks in a White House staff member— also in moderation—is loyalty. A loyal advisor is obedient and discreet. The president's trust in his loyalty grows slowly, often over years of close association. When the trust is sufficient, a president can raise or solicit names, ideas, options, and sentiments for candid discussion without fear of exposure. Otherwise the temptation to use information against the president must be presumed too great. Only the trusted associate is expected to forego short-term gains, to protect the president from exposure despite disagreements of the moment, and to lend ungrudging support after the president has rejected his advice.

In excess, loyalty in the White House turns into flattery and canine servility. "I don't want a government of yes-men," said Richard Nixon in his campaign for the presidency, but he knew how difficult it might be to avoid. The advisor who does not tend to agree with the president in the discussions which precede decision may lose his job. It is safer to agree. Many do so thoughtlessly, others against their better judgment. Men of courage falter in the presence of the president of the land. It takes rare integrity to express honest disagreement in the White House, particularly when it is known that presidents, on the average, are sensitive and vain. There are presidents who value servility, and White House staffers are subject to sycophancy for want of the independence of means and reputation that encourages a person to put his job on the line for the sake of principle. An interesting exception was Bill Moyers, fledgling Baptist preacher from Texas, prodigy and protégé when in 1963, at twenty-nine, he went with Lyndon Johnson to the White House. He was an advisor who might be said to have outgrown his mentor by the time he left in 1967 to become a New York newspaper publisher.

Sometimes an advisor is able to bring unpopular views to the attention of the president at reduced risk by accepting responsibility for their presentation but not for their validity. By role-playing as the devil's advocate the advisor remains uncommitted to the ideas he represents. A decision to inaugurate this role occurred in the Kennedy administration as a result of the abortive invasion of Cuba in 1961. In the discussions leading to the invasion, the few who questioned the plan grew silent in the face of a developing consensus in favor of the landing. Within the White House Office, the occasional skeptic, overwhelmed by the ponderous self-confidence of the officials from the Defense and State Departments and armed services, soon retired to the periphery. One of the lessons of the Cuban disaster, therefore, was the need for safeguards against premature consensus. Said Arthur Schlesinger, "For our part, we resolved to be less acquiescent next time. The Bay of Pigs gave us a license for the impolite inquiry and the rude comment." In White House staff meetings on foreign policy thereafter McGeorge Bundy took responsibility for presenting a wider range of people and ideas, and Theodore Sorensen did as much for domestic policy.[11]

Bundy's proficiency in the role of devil's advocate seemed to mature as he continued as assistant to the president for national security affairs under Lyndon Johnson. But on the issue of the war in Vietnam, as the Pentagon Papers and other accounts of the period revealed after the fact, Bundy and his associates were almost wilfully shortsighted. Driven by a sense of mission without the self-discipline to define the mission, more prepared to make history than to profit by it, these brilliant men, who were unused to failure, ignored warning signs and advanced self-confidently and self-righteously into the military and moral quagmire of a bad war. The outward appearance was one of mastery; the reality was drift. And in support of their policies they created, in the words of one critic, "an elaborate machine to lie to them."[12]

Bundy was succeeded before long by Walt Rostow, a man who preferred to press a single point of view tenaciously. Rostow shared President Johnson's aggressiveness, his nationalism, and, according to a former associate, "his conspiratorial view of life and politics."[13] The two men reinforced one another's assumptions and withdrew progressively from the company of official and private critics of United States policy in Vietnam. The lesson of the Bay of Pigs was lost.

Devil's advocacy is difficult to attempt or to sustain. That it has been deemed important is a sign of the stifling atmosphere of the White House. Even at its best, the courageous representation of several points of view by staff members may fall short of expectations. A ritualistic presentation of minority viewpoints may have the unintended effect of confirming the majority's confidence in their liberality of outlook and in the rationality and unassailability of their decisions. On the whole the experience of advising suggests the difficulty of preventing a drift from loyalty to sycophancy.

Political scientist Alexander George has proposed a remedy—multiple advocacy—that is more thoroughgoing than devil's advocacy in combatting the tendency toward premature consensus among presidential advisors. Under this plan the president would direct the creation and maintenance of a number of well-staffed, conflicting centers of analysis in the executive, all roughly equal in knowledge, analytical resources, bargaining skills, and influence. Different points of view would be nurtured and protected to assure a serious consideration of alternatives instead of a pro forma review characteristic of devil's advocacy. And should these centers of advocacy be unable to offer an appropriate range of views on any question, the president would be prepared to call in outsiders or to assign members of the White House staff to advocate further alternatives.[14] Multiple advocacy would not appeal to all presidents, but it might well reduce the incidence of one-sided advice for some.

To most recruits, service in the White House seems incomparably attractive. There are costs, certainly, but they tend to be subtle and slow to mature. An invitation to the White House Office is likely to be accepted. Later on, if costs outweigh benefits, the presidential assistant leaves.

Among the rewards of working on the White House staff are power, prestige, and inside information. Sometimes the power and prestige exceed that of the head of an agency. Even concealed from public view, members of the White House Office are feared and respected in Washington. Efforts are made to keep all but the press secretary out of the limelight; they rarely make public statements. Once in a while precautions are so elaborate that one infers the presence of a skeleton in the White House closet. Richard Nixon's skeletons were Murray Chotiner and Harry Dent, the one a political advisor from the old days in California who had helped Nixon win a reputation as a no-holds-barred campaigner, and the other a protégé of Senator Strom Thurmond of South Carolina, a symbol of President Nixon's debt to southern whites in the election of 1968. Both were kept under heavy wraps in the White House.

The internal and external information White House staff members acquire is a powerful psychic reward. For articulate presidential assistants it is what best sellers are made of—when the time comes.

White House Office salaries are not an important consideration one way or the other. They are comfortable, below the level some can command in private life and a step up for others. For the unestablished young person the president chooses as his close associate, the prospect of working in the White House is supremely attractive.

But costs of White House service prove high for some. Dismissal occurs at the whim of the president, who need not be worried about offending a constituency as he does in the case of cabinet officials. As an alternative the unfortunate assistant may be kept on the payroll but ignored on all questions of importance. If the president is jealous of his advisors, in the tradition of Franklin Roosevelt and Lyndon Johnson, he will not be above scheming to keep them in their place. The most serious penalties, which a number of souls have endured for years, are personal abuse by the president and scapegoating by the public. Eric Goldman has described the relations of Lyndon Johnson and his staff as feudal. The president, says Goldman, poked into everything, made personal suggestions about the appearance and deportment of his assistants, berated them liberally and praised them inordinately.[15] He was a harsh leader, widely regarded among his acquaintances as a man who used people and, if necessary, used them up.

Franklin Roosevelt had a similar reputation for selfishness and cruelty in his relations with subordinates, although his subtlety and charm spared him the personal criticism Johnson received from all sides. He allowed the men around him to draw fire from critics of the New Deal without coming to their defense. Harry Hopkins was depicted as Rasputin; Tugwell as "Rex the Red," a Communist, a fascist, a traitor, a Lenin, and a madman; and Tommy Corcoran was the fixer and the arm twister by popular account while Roosevelt kept aloof.[16] When an assistant had been accused of more than his quota of troublemaking, Roosevelt let him go unceremoniously. Tugwell's reputation was hurt so much by popular suspicions and tall tales that he was unable to return to Columbia University after his government service. For a time he was reduced to working for a molasses company. Lyndon Johnson's assistant, Walt Rostow, had an equally difficult transition to private life. Spurned by his former colleagues at M.I.T. for his part in the Vietnam war, Rostow retreated to the University of Texas and the continuing protection of Lyndon Johnson. To end one's public career as a scapegoat is a disheartening prospect and must be counted as a grave risk of service in the White House.

In the Nixon administration, noted for the loyalty and cohesion of its inner circle, there was an epidemic of scapegoating as the Watergate story unfolded. Present and former officials rushed to implicate one another, each in a vain effort to cleanse himself of suspicion, and the president abruptly changed his position from a denial of White House complicity to an assurance that he would personally ferret out guilty members of his staff. When the charges grew too serious and concrete for discretion to prevail, there was a general falling out among the members of the team.

All of the hopes and fears of advisor and president are found in the career of Henry Kissinger, advisor to Presidents Kennedy, Johnson, and Nixon, successor to Bundy and Rostow, and a presidential intimate in the tradition of Col. House, Harry Hopkins, and Sherman Adams. Early in his career Kissinger listed the frustrations inherent in the advisory relationship—and years later fell into an entente with President Nixon as if to prove that a Harvard intellectual and a pragmatist in the White House could transact despite them. By Kissinger's dour account, policy-making in the executive branch tends to be aimless and sterile. Bureaucrats seek outside advice in order to overcome their insecurities and the drift of institutional consensus. They invite advisors to Washington on the wrong terms—to endorse established solutions or at most to solve problems rather than to contribute to the more serious work of defining the problems.

Kissinger's advice to would-be advisors was to avoid the two dangers of submitting to the government's definition of the relevant and heading so far off in the other direction as to be too abstract to be of practical use. As Nixon's advisor, Kissinger clearly did not err on the side of abstraction.

Family and Cronies

The most consistently loyal and detached advisors of all are cronies and members of the family. Their special intimacy and mutual trust with the president develop over years of social exchange, with few of the strains of subordination and ambition found in advisory relations in general. Family and cronies may be appointed to the cabinet, the White House Office, or other official positions, or to none at all, but their relation to the president is largely informal. Robert Kennedy was attorney general in the administration of John Kennedy and widely considered an heir to the presidency as well, but what mattered most in his role of advisor to the president was that he was a close member of the family. He would have been almost as useful as an advisor if he had been in private law practice a mile from the White House.

Not all presidents need close advisors for the same reason. Some needs are compensatory: a president turns to intimates for advice when his formal advisory bodies prove intractable or untrustworthy; another uses the warmth and approval of family and friends as a brace against a harsh world. For Franklin Roosevelt, who coveted information and opinion from every quarter, contacts with intimates were part of a well-rounded system of give and take rather than a symptom of institutional or personal weakness. Indeed, if Roosevelt had emotional requirements that family and friends could satisfy, they were well hidden. He remained an actor, with a winning mixture of dignity, gregariousness, and self-confidence, "a man of superior but impenetrable mind," according to the psychologist Jung. Roosevelt was never close to others inside or outside the family, unless perhaps at times to his dearest companions, Lucy Mercer Rutherford and Marguerite Le-Hand.

The most significant family advisors in this century have been of the president's generation—wives and brothers. Edith Wilson, Eleanor

Roosevelt, Lady Bird Johnson, Milton Eisenhower, and Robert Kennedy comprised a roster of strong-willed and talented people who could treat a president of the United States as an equal. Sons have been helpful but not important in the affairs of the White House. Franklin Roosevelt hired his son James as an aide for a time and Dwight Eisenhower his son John. When the generational difference ran the other way, in the case of Roosevelt's mother, Sara Delano Roosevelt, there is little evidence of a significant exchange. The imperious Sara gave her son the president a good deal of unsolicited advice on affairs of state, but he ignored it.

Cronies, like members of the family, may become valued advisors if the president needs them for political advice more than he needs a

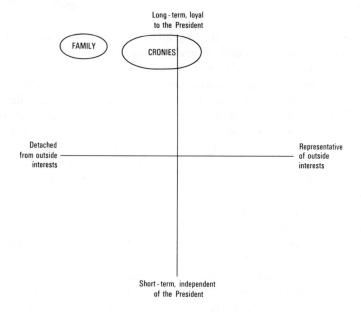

retreat from politics into the congeniality of golf or poker. Strong and weak presidents alike have had their cronies—Andrew Jackson his Kitchen Cabinet, which gave him advice of a directness and objectivity far surpassing that of the official cabinet; Harry Truman his Missouri Gang; Eisenhower his bridge team; and Richard Nixon his circle of self-made millionaires.

Family and cronies are desirable as presidential advisors for several reasons. They are loyal. Whether in the privacy of their minds they feel unreserved devotion to the president as a friend, husband, or brother, they are disinclined to go against him in a moment of disillusionment. A falling out ends the transaction without denunciations and public embarrassment. Their trustful exchanges with the president permit a degree of candor that other advisors rarely attain. Detached from outside interests too, and peculiarly adept at understanding the president's problems, they are notably free of parochial biases, though they may be people of stature in their own right, as were Milton Eisenhower and Eleanor Roosevelt, and they pose no threat as empire builders or subversives. Mrs. Roosevelt was exceptional in a number of respects: humane and intelligent, increasingly independent of an unloving husband, and the friend and representative of organized labor and other minorities, a worldly person with a good understanding of the interests surrounding the presidency.

The disadvantages in using cronies and family as political advisors are twofold: a limited selection and the inevitable charges of cronyism and nepotism. Modern presidents who appoint intimates to advisory posts are not, in fact, dispensing old-fashioned patronage. It is safe to say that Robert Kennedy did not need the attorney general's salary. But President-elect John Kennedy, flinching in advance from the criticism he anticipated, mused with a friend about a discreet announcement of the appointment of the attorney general: "I think I'll open the door . . . about 2:00 A.M., look up and down the street, and, if there's no one there, I'll whisper, 'It's Bobby.' "[17] In any event the costs of advice from intimates are likely to be obvious at the time of the initial exchange. With other advisors the costs tend to be subtle and progressive.

From the standpoint of the crony or member of the family, the advantages of serving the president are almost certain to outweigh the costs—the president will not often be turned down. His intimates have ties of affection, first of all. And they have little or nothing to lose by increasing their contact with him. For a crony of modest talent, a connection with the White House promises an escape from a humdrum life. Harry Vaughan was a struggling tea salesman when he hitched himself to Harry Truman. He advanced from assistant in the Senate to military aide in the White House with the rank of brigadier general, sadly out of place, wheeling and dealing, an embarrassment to the nation, but a friend and comfort to his president. When the alternative is to peddle tea, working for the president of the United States is a good bargain. Cronies of independent standing have little to lose either, for different reasons. A millionaire whose reputation is secured against criticism by his net worth at most adds or loses a feather in his cap by his association, or by ending his association, with the president.[18]

The rise of family and old friends to the rank of advisor is more a matter of luck than merit. Presidents make use of them most often because of the difficulty of getting good advisors, particularly loyal ones, through other channels. Their presence is a reflection on the institution of the presidency. It is the good fortune of the nation that a fair number of these men and women, these accidents of family and friendship, have proved extraordinarily able.

Task Forces and White House Conferences

Loyalty and detachment are necessary in a presidential advisory system, but they are not sufficient. For fresh thinking or political and social intelligence, the modern chief executive is likely to turn to task forces and an occasional White House conference. Task forces, in addition, are a source of general advice in the months between a president's

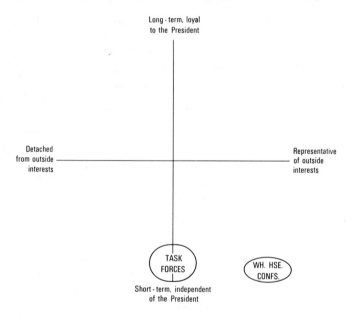

election and his assumption of office. White House conferences represent outside interests; loyalty is neither necessary nor desirable. Both task forces and conferences give short-term advice, and they are singularly independent of the president.

John Kennedy recruited twenty-nine task forces on foreign and domestic problems to report to him by inauguration day. All but five met the deadline. Men such as J. K. Galbraith, Walt Rostow, Seymour Harris, and Paul Douglas volunteered their services to assess the pressing issues of the day for the guidance of the new president and his cabinet.[19] Lyndon Johnson appointed a new set of task forces upon his succession to the presidency. By 1967 there were about fifty in operation, some with outsiders, some with government people, and some mixed. President Johnson made two changes from the Kennedy pattern: fewer intellectuals and a cloak of secrecy—for practical reasons and because he disliked intellectuals and liked secrecy.[20] Recruiting men of affairs would result in more realism in the reports, he felt, and secrecy would protect his options. He was skeptical of presidential commissions, which sometimes studied endlessly without result or, worse, published conclusions embarrassing to the president—the liberal Kerner Commission on urban riots and the Douglas Commission on urban problems were cases in point. A secret report might be ignored with impunity or considered at leisure without premature criticism by members of the opposition.

White House conferences are convened on topics of public interest, such as civil rights and the problems of youth. They bring many individual and organizational viewpoints into discussion groups and plenary sessions with the possibility of reaching some consensus. Their central purpose is political, however. They express White House concern about a set of problems, establish ties with disaffected interests, and soften differences among them. But a number of conferences have, above all, provided a forum for critics of White House policy, and a few have exploded. Lyndon Johnson, after one rowdy conference, was heard to vow it would be the last. Still they go on, and they are a source of intelligence for the president, not on fine points of policy but on the feelings, and the intensity of the feelings, of people affected by federal policy. It took a White House conference to inform President Johnson of the depth of black dissatisfaction with the theorizing of then Assistant Secretary of Labor Daniel Patrick Moynihan, who seemed to be suggesting that blacks were more in need of family reform than of civil rights legislation.

A president needs advice from task forces and conferences because of the fixed commitments and limited vision of his regular advisors. Only short-term advisors, perhaps including some bureaucrats on special assignment, are sufficiently free of political inhibitions to turn out new ideas and blunt assessments of old ones. Only they are likely to argue a case straightforwardly, without consciously or unconsciously promoting the special interests of some agencies of government over others. The two disadvantages to the president are the possibility that the advice will be impractical and that publication of a set of recommendations will give the appearance of presidential sanction to views which may not be his. Lyndon Johnson's innovations reduce these costs.

For the citizen called to advise the president in one of these capacities, the gain is likely to exceed the possible loss. There is public service of importance, a sense of participation in affairs of state, possibly some personal contact with the president, and no danger of a serious fall from grace—no dismissal, no public ridicule. The only disadvantages, which are slight, are that he may be pledged to anonymity and his advice may be ignored.

Less-Defined Advisory Roles

Most advisory transactions are fairly well defined, but a few advisors and advisory bodies are ambiguous, because their functions are diffuse or because the advisors migrate from one role to another. A good example is Franklin Roosevelt's "Brain Trust." A group with some of the qualities of a task force, it was assembled during the 1932 campaign at the suggestion of Roosevelt's friend and speech writer, Sam Rosenman, to advise the candidate on national issues. Three professors from Columbia University, Raymond Moley, Rex Tugwell, and Adolph A. Berle, Jr., were the core—men of talent and intellect who offered the president a generous fare of ideas, each from a different philosophical position. The president, once described as a man with a flypaper mind, gained a certain sophistication in economic affairs from the group and some good speeches for the campaign trail.

After the election the members of the Brain Trust continued to serve the president in official and unofficial capacities without ever again working as a group. Their importance to Roosevelt increased steadily, though just how powerful the Brain Trust became in setting national policy is a point upon which historians still differ. Some of Roosevelt's detractors were convinced that he was the captive of a coterie of radical professors. As the president's confidence in them grew, the members of the Brain Trust assumed positions akin to those of senior White House staff in later administrations. Yet because they had strong ideas of their own, the exchange was uneasy, and before long most of the Brain Trust had fallen out with Roosevelt. They exhibited the same volatile combination of independence, feigned detachment, and irrepressible representation of interests that drove Daniel Patrick Moynihan from the White House a generation later.

The Council of Economic Advisors, a grandchild of the Brain Trust, has had a comparable history of unsettled relations with the president. Created in the Executive Office of the President by the Employment Act of 1946, the council was a symbol of the determination of Congress to bring the economic advisory function into the open and to keep future presidents from putting together shadowy ad hoc groups like the Brain

Trust. The Employment Act required Senate confirmation of members of the council, in contrast to the exemption of the principal officers of its sister agency, the Bureau of the Budget, as it was then known. The implication was that the director of the bureau and his assistants were the president's men, but the members of the Council of Economic Advisors were responsible jointly to the president and Congress, a responsibility reinforced by the requirement of an annual report to Congress.

The economic advisors divided their allegiance during the remainder of Harry Truman's administration, and the president, therefore, was inclined to draw economic advice from John Steelman, Clark Clifford, and others outside the council. Under Eisenhower, Kennedy, and Johnson, the council entered the presidential orbit and grew more reserved with Congress. Members of the council remained silent when the president rejected their advice. They were loyal and detached, but unlike White House staff members retained a sense of professionalism as economists, and might be known for individual views and favorite remedies not inconsistent with the program of the president. A final identification of the council with the White House occurred in 1972, when the chairman campaigned for the reelection of President Nixon, along with the Secretaries of Defense and State and the Director of the FBI, all of whom by custom had been expected to remain aloof from political campaigns.

Like the White House Office and the cabinet, the Council of Economic Advisors sometimes is useful to the president as a scapegoat. Said Kennedy to council chairman Walter Heller, doing loyal service as the administration's butt of economic criticism, "Walter, I want to make it perfectly clear that I resent these attacks on you." The president, of course, had no intention of coming to his defense.

Restricted Advice under Certain Presidents

Whatever the uses to which they are put by the president, advisors of many talents stand ready to serve the White House today. A strong, open president who needs ideas to fuel his political ambitions and is receptive to advice from disparate sources can run a complex advisory system. A less ambitious president or one, ambitious or not, who trusts few of his associates, has less advice and less chance of succeeding as president. Active presidents tend to emulate the openness of Franklin Roosevelt.

But some presidents have depended heavily on a few advisors as a result of internal or external forces—a president grows distrustful of all but his most loyal aides, for example, or avoids the hazards of broad consultation under the pressures of time and secrecy in a moment of crisis. Of presidents who have preferred a small group of advisors even in the absence of crisis, Woodrow Wilson is the clearest illustration. His intense need for approval and affection was the legacy of a childhood in which he absorbed high standards of conduct in unusually threatening circumstances. Through his entire life, Wilson strove for excellence and received global recognition as a scholar and statesman without overcoming his fear of failure or his vulnerability to the kind of criticism he had suffered in the family. No one aroused Wilson's primal anxieties to better advantage than Senator Henry Cabot Lodge, who humiliated the president with zest and invention, once even ridiculing his prose as Wilson's father had long before. Committed antagonists were not the only ones who stirred up old troubles in Wilson, however. He was acutely sensitive to disagreement and other signs of disloyalty in men he met in the normal routine of office, and could talk comfortably about important matters only with people whose ultimate approval was assured. Aside from friends and family, few were thought trustworthy, and good friends no less than others had to learn the dangers of disagreement. There came a time when the only ones he trusted were his wife and Col. House, and then his wife alone.

House was loyal and supportive as Wilson's principal advisor on domestic and foreign affairs, partly by natural inclination and partly by guile. He had an old preference for staying in the shadows, an "almost Oriental modesty, a Chinese self-effacement,"[21] to which he added a studied sycophancy for the benefit of Wilson, praising him endlessly, conveying the praises of others, and agreeing without fail. Only with House, the cynic and manipulator, did the president feel enough at ease to relax his self-control and express his deeper feelings. For years House turned away official appointments and interviews with the press in order not to give an appearance of sharing Wilson's glory. When at last he relented and allowed himself an official title, an interview, and a difference of opinion with the president, all within a short period, House fell irrevocably from favor.

The only successor with a Wilsonian appetite for sycophancy was Lyndon Johnson. As one of his aides reminisced, "Any president has to have around him some people who are so unquestioningly loyal that their very loyalty is a source of strength." To the delight of the press and the country, another aide, Jack Valenti, aired his loyalty in public: "He is a sensitive man, a cultivated man, a warmhearted and extraordinary man. . . . I sleep each night a little better, a little more confidently, because Lyndon Johnson is my president."[22] It is normal for a president, as for anyone else, to want support and affection from those about him. What sets a Wilson or a Johnson apart is the intensity of the requirement, the emotional immaturity it implies, and the dramatic loss of contact it causes with the world beyond.

**Restricted Advice in
Time of Crisis**

A narrowing of the circle of advisors is at times the product of events rather than a sign of dependency. There are crises inside and outside the White House which by custom or law place heavy burdens on a few advisors and displace the rest. When crisis occurs in the administration of a president who consults few advisors normally, the narrowing may be severe.

There is no more critical event in the White House than the disability of the chief executive. It disrupts advisory relationships and engenders uncertainty and mutual distrust. Two courses of action are open to the people around the president: to carry on in his name, with whatever contributions the president can make, or to replace him with an acting president under the terms of the Twenty-fifth Amendment. In either case the president's advisors must exercise great power.

Woodrow Wilson's disabling stroke in September, 1919, left him utterly dependent, personally and politically, on his wife and physician. For months only they and consulting physicians saw the president. It was Mrs. Wilson who decided what matters would be brought to his attention and she, therefore, who set executive priorities. The president's doctors were agreed that resignation from office would further jeopardize his health. The vice-president, for his part, stayed well in the background for fear of seeming to be a usurper. The presidency thus remained in limbo for one and a half years, Wilson a cripple amidst gossip about his insanity and death and Mrs. Wilson in large degree president de facto.

When he suffered a heart attack in 1955, Dwight Eisenhower had the benefit of Wilson's example. He and his close advisors were resolved not to be secretive in the event of disability, a resolve that was honored, more or less, in the illnesses that followed. Press Secretary Hagerty was responsible for translating medical reports into lay language when the heart attack occurred, but he added a penchant for theatrics that affected public confidence in his news releases. The illness also gave Hagerty powers that rivaled Mrs. Wilson's for a time. He was the only official to see the president and interpret his state of mind to the outside world for nearly a week.[23] Since neither the illness nor the monopoly on advising lasted as it had in Wilson's administration, history has been gentler with Hagerty than with Mrs. Wilson. The medical crises of the Eisenhower years revived public interest in a legal remedy.

The Twenty-fifth Amendment, ratified in 1967, was meant to replace the tradition of vice-presidential reticence and ad hoc transactions involving one or two key advisors during disability by creating fixed procedures for vesting the powers of the presidency in the vice-president. The president himself, we know from experience, cannot be trusted any more than his intimates to turn to the vice-president. Indeed, in the case of Wilson, there is evidence of a kind of brain damage which produces a pattern of strong denial of one's disability and peculiar symbolic references to matters relating to the illness.[24] Wilson even desired, vainly, a third term as president in his pitiable condition. With the support of a majority of the cabinet, the vice-president, according to the Twenty-fifth Amendment, is empowered to make a finding of presidential disability and take over, subject to appeal by the president to Congress. The cabinet, which had been brushed aside in disability crises in the past, now has been given an important role in returning power when his health is restored. The cabinet is both close to the president and responsive to outside interests, a mixture of qualities that makes an objective decision seem reasonably likely. The Twenty-fifth Amendment does permit Congress to put another body, perhaps experts of some description, in the place of the cabinet to make the disability decision. But the wisdom of relying on experts for worldly judgments about presidents was cast in question in 1964 when the editor of *Fact* magazine asked 12,356 psychiatrists, "Is Barry Goldwater psychologically fit to be President of the United States?" and received 2,417 responses, surprisingly. Of these, 1,189 said no, 657 said yes, and 571 had the sense to admit they lacked the information to make a professional judgment. The magazine carried forty-one pages of sensational diagnosis volunteered by the respondents, a better indication of the mental state of the minority of psychiatrists who answered, perhaps, than of the candidate.[25] The country might long for a return to pre-Twenty-fifth Amendment expedients if such a blend of hunch and spite were ever put in practice by a disability board.

Crises occurring outside the White House, particularly international crises, tend to result in more intense exchanges with fewer advisors than usual. As in the case of presidential disability, a handful of advisors who are not necessarily the most able may abruptly find themselves exercising enormous power.

Confronted with the threat or the fact of sudden international violence, a president will likely ignore statutory consultative mechanisms and put together an ad hoc group of advisors, small at first while major choices are made and more numerous as technical questions of implementation arise. The need for full information and the representation of all significant points of view before a decision is made tend to be outweighed in crisis by pressures to keep the number of advisors small for the sake of secrecy, dispatch, and flexibility, and by an emotional need to be physically close to a select, supportive few. Experience indicates that information available to the president is reduced by the narrowing of his circle of advisors. Also, less obviously, it is lessened by the tendency of people under stress to fall back on old facts and old assumptions even in the face of contradictory intelligence, and to be less willing than ever to challenge hierarchical authority.[26]

If rational decision-making requires thorough fact-finding, the crisis behavior of presidents leaves much to be desired. Of course, the reverse may be true, as Theodore Lowi has suggested: clearance and consultation with salient interests may have led to a politics of stagnation from which the decisiveness of crisis is a welcome relief.[27]

John Kennedy, according to his friendlier biographers, suffered from inadequate advice in the early days of his administration, and learned his lesson. The pull of one-sided advice, notably in discussions preceding the invasion of Cuba in 1961, was at first compounded by his habit of immersing himself in detail, then finding himself swept along with the drift of his advisors' opinion. But when the second Cuban crisis occurred the following year a seasoned John Kennedy assembled a larger group with diverse viewpoints and stayed aloof from most of their deliberations in order to be uncommitted as long as possible and to discourage his advisors from telling him what they thought he might want to hear.[28] For the same reason Harry Truman did not attend meetings of the National Security Council, which was established during his time in office.

Richard Nixon evolved a style of decision-making that exaggerated the normal isolation of presidents during crisis, taking counsel from one man, frequently, and retiring afterwards for a spell of lonely introspection and a decision. He spent much of his time in Maryland, Florida, and California retreats. The result was an interesting, erratic administration with incredible blunders and a few bold successes. If he had imitated his mentor, General Eisenhower, President Nixon's decisions would have been more institutional than personal, and more predictable.

Still, it may not be clear whether a given decision is personal or institutional. John Kennedy's decision-making in the Cuban missile crisis, often cited as an example of the effective use of advisors—expertise, diversity of outlook, and candor—can also be explained as the intuitive act of a president as remote from consultants as a Richard Nixon struggling with himself in an inner study. Perhaps Kennedy proved himself a master psychologist by divining a firm but delicate course between belligerence and weakness that induced Khrushchev, without humiliation, to remove his missiles from the island. A less flattering explanation is that Kennedy was less therapist than patient: confronting an adversary who had broken a promise, his self-esteem was so endangered that the only choice of which he was capable was an abrupt reaction to restore the status quo. The basic decision to force the removal of Soviet missiles, according to this view, was made immediately and personally by the president and the consultation that followed was confined to questions of means, such as the relative merits of invasion, air strikes, and quarantine.[29]

Whatever the best account of the crisis, President Kennedy clearly shared with Woodrow Wilson and Richard Nixon a preference for the advice of one or a few souls in time of stress and a tendency to make critical decisions with no advice at all. Thus the abnormally intense exchange with abnormally few advisors occurring in time of presidential disability, international turmoil, and crisis of other kinds is not very different from acting without advice at all.

The Problem of the Vice-Presidency

Even a gregarious president in untroubled times is likely to have a cautious, meticulously defined exchange with one official—the vice-president. A vice-presidential candidate is selected by the presidential candidate with the November election in mind. He is expected to balance and strengthen the ticket. Despite the rhetoric about candidates for vice-president as right-hand men and worthy successors, the concern in nearly every modern instance has been to build a winning electoral coalition by running pairs who represent different factions within the party.

As a result, the vice-president is unlikely to see eye to eye with the president on questions of policy. He is at best a necessary evil from the president's point of view. After the election he is a threat to the president unless he can be kept in the background—the older tradition—or bound to loyalty and acquiescence in the performance of his role of apprentice—the recent tendency.

In this transaction the candidate for the presidency needs a person for the second position who will be of help to him in one or more elections and perhaps with Congress, a person of some prominence, therefore, possibly a competitor for the presidential nomination. He thus needs one who is content to take an oath of fealty and endure the indignities of the office—ridicule in public and private for accepting a role of abject subordination (a puppet, frequently, in political cartoons), exclusion from important decisions at the whim of the president, and the risk of irreversible damage to his career.[30] The candidate for the presidency is in a position to minimize costs by setting the terms of the exchange, a necessary precaution since the vice-president is the one associate who cannot be dismissed during a four-year term of office, although he can be replaced at election time. There is some resemblance between the businesslike, contractual promise of loyalty in this case and the association of men of disparate persuasion and tempera-

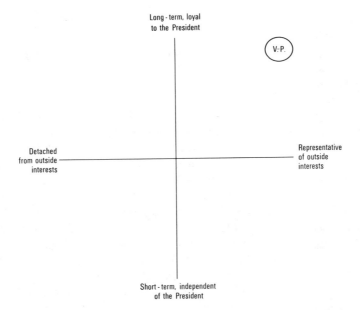

ment under the constraints of collective responsibility in the British cabinet. It is an explicit agreement to suppress differences for the duration of the regime in the expectation of mutual gain.

The candidate for the vice-presidency has one benefit in mind, which must override all costs if he is to allow himself to be nominated. That is, of course, the hope of being president one day. Once in a while a politician may adjudge himself better off becoming vice-president, it is true. Richard Nixon may have considered the vice-presidency a promotion from his position of freshman senator in 1952. But more often modern vice-presidents have accepted demotion to that post in the hope of succeeding to the presidency upon the death or permanent disability of the incumbent or by nomination and election as heir apparent. The costs are greater by far than those incurred by other presidential associates, but the prize is greater too, and not beyond reach. Of the presidents since Franklin Roosevelt, Truman, Johnson, and Nixon all were once vice-presidents.

Since vice-presidents may one day be president, recent presidents have made an effort to involve them in political and administrative activities. It was one of Franklin Roosevelt's vice-presidents, John Garner, who said the office was "not worth a pitcher of warm spit," and another, Harry Truman, who was so ill-informed of what had transpired in the White House that he was unaware of the atom bomb project until he became president. Truman's vice-president, Alben Barkley, was in his seventies, a beloved raconteur, but hardly an important figure in the administration. Eisenhower instituted the practice— or rather revived an old expedient of the Wilson and Harding administrations—of giving the vice-president executive duties, a precedent expanded in recent administrations. Lyndon Johnson as vice-president attended cabinet and National Security Council meetings, breakfasts with legislative leaders, and other important gatherings in the White House.

Yet vice-presidents since 1952 have suffered criticism without a fair chance to respond. Republican Vice-Presidents Nixon and Agnew were employed in unsavory political assignments by their chiefs, each of whom feigned nonpartisanship and encouraged the public to think that the vice-president spoke for himself. Once exploited in this manner by a genial President Eisenhower in the elections of 1954, Richard Nixon was primed for mid-term electioneering in his own administration. In 1970 Vice-President Agnew, with White House prompting and technical support, was loosed to wage a tough law-and-order campaign reminiscent of Nixon's antisubversion speeches in 1954. When Agnew's approach faltered and the election results proved disappointing, the White House let him take the blame. Once again, as in the 1950s, rumors circulated that the vice-president had gone sour and would be replaced in the next presidential election. If the treatment of Agnew seemed harsh, one might recall that in 1952, 1956, and 1960 Dwight Eisenhower had seemed in genuine doubt about Richard Nixon's fitness for office, and throughout his administration had declined to accept his vice-president as an intimate, politically or socially. Democratic vice-presidents' disabilities have been more personal—matters of style that seemed larger than ever in an office with so little substance. Lyndon Johnson was forgiven his rusticisms when he was running the Senate, but as vice-president in a stylish administration he acquired names on the order of "Uncle Cornpone." Hubert Humphrey the rhetorician seemed to be that and no more as vice-president, almost pathetic in his role of apologist for the war in Vietnam.

In such times the public might agree with Finley Peter Dunne's assessment of the office: "It isn't a crime exactly. Ye can't be sint to jail f'r it, but it's a kind iv a disgrace." Vice-presidents endure the anguish of office in the hope of being promoted and having the last laugh. Their transactions with presidents are tense, distrustful, and limited. The relationships of the president and the rest of his associates presume less antagonism from the outset and lack any agreement to maintain the exchange if serious differences should erupt later on. Unlike the minimal, stable exchange with a vice-president, these relations are unpredictable—they may grow, stagnate, atrophy, terminate, or even explode in public.

The Rupture of Advisory Exchanges

The interest of modern presidents in communications has led to the recruitment of people skilled in the uses of language for White House and cabinet posts. The president is surrounded, inescapably, by those whose talents in reaching the public through the mass media can be turned against him in the event of a rift. Other chief executives do not have this problem. Governors and mayors rarely have outstanding writers on their staffs, and the public is less curious about inside stories from city halls and state capitals.

The president's challenge is to encourage his subordinates' writing and speaking as members of the team while minimizing hurtful leaks and exposés, including unflattering books and articles published after he leaves office. He may inhibit a few subordinates by exacting a pledge not to write or tell about White House personalities and conversations, a condition of employment in the executive mansion in the Kennedy administration. But Sorensens and Schlesingers will not accept demeaning terms of employment. Their discretion depends upon continuing loyalty. *Kennedy* and *A Thousand Days* prove that the president's trust was well placed.

President Kennedy wanted Schlesinger's post as special assistant to be a vantage point for the preparation of an official history of his administration. An admirer of Schlesinger's friendly biographies of Andrew Jackson and Franklin Roosevelt, John Kennedy picked him as the historian most likely to do the same for his own presidency. But not understanding the special implications of his appointment, Schlesinger hesitated to take notes in the White House until the President gave him clear instructions during the secret discussions about the Bay of Pigs invasion.

The usual expectation is that presidential advisors will use some care in their utterances during and after their service. But in the absence of firm laws and traditions such as those of the British, which bind advisors to secrecy, indiscretions will occur. It is interesting that in Canada, despite British forms and trappings, the relation of the prime minister and his associates has much in common with American practice. A member of the cabinet who felt that Prime Minister Trudeau was paying insufficient attention to the advice of ordinary members of the cabinet resigned in 1971 and offered the press a bitter, detailed account of his reasons.[31]

An exposé of the presidency by an insider is assured a wide and eager audience. *The Ordeal of Power,* a trenchant volume on the Eisenhower administration written in the early sixties by an occasional speech writer, journalist Emmet John Hughes, revealed cabinet debates and other confidential information unflattering to the president and his advisors.[32] Hughes mixed the good with the bad, but on balance his book is the story of his own dashed hopes and of a president he could liken to Neville Chamberlain. "A kiss and tell book," one reviewer called it. Two former presidential advisors attacked *The Ordeal of Power* as the kind of breach of confidence that could dry up candor in the White House.[33] Eric Goldman, Princeton professor and White House intellectual in the Johnson administration, wrote an equally unfriendly book on his experiences and observations as an outsider in the White House. When he resigned, promising a book, the administration pointedly failed to take notice except to suggest that Professor Goldman may have worked more for Lady Bird than for the president. *The Tragedy of Lyndon Johnson,* like the work of another disillusioned Johnson assistant, George Reedy's *The Twilight of the Presidency,* is acid and entertaining, but neither is as revealing, and therefore as deadly, as *The Ordeal of Power.*

The parting shot from President Nixon's first secretary of the interior, Walter Hickel, was fired with effect before he left office. He will be remembered as the entrepreneur from Alaska who overcame the concerted opposition of the conservationists to win Senate confirmation, and within a year was their champion in Washington. As secretary he was astounded by White House attitudes about his department, young people, and the war in Indochina. But the president was inaccessible—in their first sixteen months in office Hickel was able to see him only twice. Angered and frustrated, Hickel wrote the president a blunt letter which focused on the concerns of youth and criticized the administration for ignoring their protests and attacking their motives. He concluded, "Permit me to suggest that you consider meeting, on an individual and conversational basis, with members of your cabinet.

Perhaps through such conversations we can gain greater insight into the problems confronting us all, and most important, into the solutions of these problems.[34] Copies of Secretary Hickel's letter were distributed to his aides and reprinted in the newspapers before the original reached the White House—it was generally assumed that the publication of the letter was not unexpected. Hickel was snubbed by the White House and then, at its convenience, fired.

But the removal of Walter Hickel was not the end of President Nixon's difficulties with dissident subordinates. Immediately after the publication of the secret Pentagon Papers on the escalation of the war in Vietnam, with their revelations of the duplicity of previous administrations, current information from the National Security Council began to leak to the press, culminating in the publication of the so-called White House Papers on United States policy toward India and Pakistan. These documents had been given to syndicated columnist Jack Anderson by one or more anonymous members of the council staff. It was revealed that employees of the White House office on special assignment and the FBI had worked for months to tighten security in the National Security Council without success. The White House Papers showed different private and public positions on the conflict leading to the secession of East Pakistan, notably the inconsistency in statements of presidential assistant Henry Kissinger. The revelations exacerbated the mutual distrust of the president and some of his advisors, as well as of the president and the public.

In the second term even greater dissension occurred in the White House among those implicated in the Watergate affair. The bonds of loyalty dissolved at the point at which reputations seemed likely to be ruined by further mutual solicitude. Before long a troubled nation was to witness a former presidential counsel, John Dean, in televised testimony before the Ervin investigating committee, accuse the president of feloniously participating in the Watergate cover-up.

Conclusion

Presidents in search of advisors must come to terms with a wide variety of men and women. In the ordinary course of events they interact to mutual advantage. If not, the exchanges are terminated. But in some cases the transaction goes awry and one or both of the parties bestow unpleasantness and embarrassment instead of positive rewards. Leaks, angry departures, and critical memoirs by subordinates contrast with the loyal service and clean breaks of the British political system.

There are other differences. Advisors in the United States are more specialized, as we have seen, harder to recruit because there is no reservoir of political and administrative subordinates with a proper combination of loyalty and expertise, and less reliable because of the absence of enforceable standards of discretion.

The options for an American chief executive, therefore, are to exploit the pluralism and openness of the political culture in the manner of Franklin Roosevelt, accepting advice from all quarters in and out of government and encouraging competitiveness among advisors, or to retreat from the risks entailed in maintaining advisory transactions and rely increasingly on the counsel of trusted associates, as in the administration of Richard Nixon. The ways of these two presidents are typified by their different treatment of their secretaries of the interior: Roosevelt's Ickes and Nixon's Hickel were both blunt, idealistic, combative men, often at odds with the White House, and characteristically ignored by the president for long periods. Yet Ickes was a valued member of the Roosevelt entourage, and Hickel, for the same reasons, a cancer to be excised at the first politic opportunity.

NOTES

[1]For example, Theodore C. Sorensen, *Kennedy* (New York: Harper & Row, Publishers, 1965), p. 254; Richard Fenno, *The President's Cabinet* (New York: Vintage Books, 1959), pp. 30, 63. Compare David Halberstam, *The Best and the Brightest* (New York: Random House, Inc., 1972), a critical account of White House advising by "the best."

[2]My account of the cabinet borrows liberally from Fenno.

[3]Dwight D. Eisenhower, *Mandate for Change* (Garden City, N.Y.: Doubleday & Co., Inc., 1963), p. 91. Copyright 1963 by Doubleday & Co., Inc.

[4]Thomas E. Cronin, " 'Everybody Believes in Democracy Until He Gets to the White House . . .': An Examination of White House-Departmental Relations," *Law and Contemporary Problems,* XXXV, No. 3 (1970), 613–16.

[5]Sorensen, *Kennedy,* p. 254.

[6]Fenno, *The President's Cabinet,* pp. 101–2.

[7]*Ibid.,* p. 137.

[8]"How Nixon's White House Works," *Time,* June 8, 1970, p. 18.

[9]George Reedy, *The Twilight of the Presidency* (New York: The New American Library, Inc., 1970).

[10]*New York Times,* May 14, 1970, p. 20.

[11]Arthur M. Schlesinger, Jr., *A Thousand Days* (Boston: Houghton Mifflin Company, 1965), p. 297; Sorensen, *Kennedy,* p. 282.

[12]Halberstam, *The Best and the Brightest,* pp. 527, 595–96, 635, 655.

[13]Townsend Hoopes, *The Limits of Intervention* (New York: David McKay Co., Inc., 1969), pp. 60–61.

[14]Alexander L. George, "The Case for Multiple Advocacy in Making Foreign Policy," *American Political Science Review*, LXVI, No. 3 (1972), 751–85.

[15]Eric Goldman, *The Tragedy of Lyndon Johnson* (New York: Dell Publishing Co., Inc., 1968), p. 120; Halberstam, *The Best and the Brightest*, p. 434.

[16]Patrick Anderson, *The Presidents' Men* (Garden City, N.Y.: Doubleday & Co., Inc., 1968), pp. 38, 61, 98.

[17]Schlesinger, *A Thousand Days*, p. 142.

[18]*New York Times*, January 17, 1970, p. 1.

[19]Schlesinger, *A Thousand Days*, pp. 159–61.

[20]Norman Thomas and Harold Wolman, "The Johnson Task Forces," in *The Presidential Advisory System*, eds. Thomas E. Cronin and Sanford Greenberg (New York: Harper & Row, Publishers, 1969), pp. 124–43.

[21]William Allen White, quoted in Alexander L. and Juliette L. George, *Woodrow Wilson and Colonel House* (New York: John Day, 1956), p. 84.

[22]Anderson, *The Presidents' Men*, pp. 382–83.

[23]*Ibid.*, pp. 222–23.

[24]Edwin A. Weinstein, "Denial of Presidential Disability," *Psychiatry*, XXX, No. 4 (1967), 376ff.

[25]*New York Times*, October 2, 1964, p. 20.

[26]Glenn D. Paige, *The Korean Decision* (New York: The Free Press, 1968), pp. 282ff.

[27]Theodore Lowi, *The End of Liberalism* (New York: W. W. Norton & Company, Inc., 1969), Chap. 3.

[28]Anderson, *The Presidents' Men*, pp. 243–44; Robert Kennedy, *Thirteen Days* (New York: W. W. Norton & Company, Inc., 1969), pp. 9, 22–23, 94–96.

[29]Edward D. Hoedemaker, "Distrust and Aggression," *Conflict Resolution*, XI, No. 1 (1968), 69ff.; Thomas M. Mongar, "Personality and Decision-Making," *Canadian Journal of Political Science*, II, No. 2 (1969), 200ff.

[30]See Halberstam, *The Best and the Brightest*, pp. 533–36, on the humiliation of Hubert Humphrey.

[31]Walter Stewart, "Baby, It Was Cold Inside," *Maclean's*, July, 1971, pp. 32, 63, 64, 66.

[32]Emmet John Hughes, *The Ordeal of Power* (New York: Atheneum Publishers, 1963).

[33]Adolph Berle and Malcolm Moos, "The Need to Know and the Right to Tell," *Political Science Quarterly*, LXXIX, No. 2 (1964), 161–83.

[34]*New York Times*, May 7, 1970, p. 18.

t
h
r
e
e

The President and the Bureaucracy

On an organization chart of the executive branch of the federal government, the president stands atop a pyramid of agencies, commissions, and armed services. The chart is reasonably accurate as a symbol of formal relationships of dominance and subordination, but as a guide to the working relationships of the president and the bureaucracy it is grossly misleading. Actual relations are determined less by the structural requirements of the Constitution and acts of Congress than by the willingness and ability of the president and the bureaucrats to engage in mutually profitable exchanges.

In the 1960s and 1970s the patterns of interaction in civilian and military programs became distinct. Presidents and the bureaucrats in civilian programs tend to have few converging interests and accordingly few exchanges. In earlier generations there were moments of intense interaction, but normally, today, presidents exert marginal influence over civilian programs, and bureaucrats in these programs are indifferent to the White House. But the president and the bureaucracy in military programs—the Pentagon and associated intelligence and paramilitary units (which together employ as many people as the civilian programs) and the uniformed military services—have attained a high level of exchange in the same period, despite the history of tensions between the two and constitutional traditions of civilian control to restrain the military from bargaining with the president. Largely because of the president, in a new milieu of unending preparation for war, the relationship has become warmer and more trustful.

There is a parallel in the president's relations with Congress. The White House has conceded responsibility for domestic policy-making to the legislature, by and large, and Congress has given effective control of foreign and military affairs to the White House, even though the Constitution calls for a sharing of authority in each case. From the president's viewpoint, domestic affairs tend to be hard fields to till, while military affairs are fertile. There are more options, fewer vested interests to excite, and a predictable surplus of public acclaim over public anxiety for each new decision made. It should be noted that foreign affairs have an ambiguous place in this scheme of things. Diplomacy is a function of special concern to the White House, over which Congress has now relinquished control. It is inseparable in practice from military affairs; but the State Department itself is estranged from the president. Modern presidents have found it as intractable as the Corps of Engineers and the Department of Agriculture. In this chapter, therefore, we shall examine the occasional interactions of the president and the State Department along with comparable examples of relations with bureaucrats in civilian programs. We shall then consider the more intense interactions of the president and his subordinates in military programs.

Normal Exchanges with Bureaucrats in Civilian Programs

The president has a number of devices with which to control people in civilian agencies. In theory he may place loyal men and women in key positions, direct their activities, and remove them if they resist his influence. In practice, however, he is likely to find the full utilization of his powers too costly. In the long run he finds it more profitable to yield to claims of bureaucratic autonomy or congressional prerogative than to expend time and resources and risk defeat in an area with few political rewards for the White House. His controls include the power to "take care that the laws be faithfully executed," the powers of appointment and removal, and the clearance of requests for appropriations and legislation by the Office of Management and Budget.

Among the presidents who have helped to broaden the power of supervising and directing the work of the agencies of the executive branch, Andrew Jackson stands out for having successfully asserted that the constitutional injunction to "take care that the laws be faithfully executed" allowed the president to overrule the head of a department. Not long before, an attorney general of the United States had held that the provision was at most a mandate to remove or to initiate proceedings against a dishonest official, and was not an excuse for doing the official's work for him.[1] President Jackson wrote:

> By the constitution "the executive power is vested in a president of the United States." Among the duties imposed upon him, and which he is sworn faithfully to perform, is that of "taking care that the laws be faithfully executed." Being thus made responsible for the entire action of the executive department, it was but reasonable that the power of appointing, overseeing, and controlling those who execute the laws—a power in its nature executive—should remain in his hands.[2]

Jackson prevailed.

Today a president may determine the course of antitrust policy during his administration or issue orders to the agencies of government concerned with school desegregation to follow his interpretation of the Constitution and civil rights laws. While many may question the prudence of his orders, few would argue that his discretionary authority is unconstitutional. The power is vast, but in normal times the president applies it selectively, in programs with which he chooses to have some special identification as, say, a trust buster or a proponent of civil rights.

He has the power to appoint "Ambassadors . . . and all other Officers of the United States whose Appointments are not . . . otherwise provided for" in the Constitution, subject to the provision that "Congress may by Law vest the Appointment of such inferior Officers, as they think proper, in the President alone, in the Courts of Law, or in the Heads of Departments."

In a number of respects, however, this is a power of limited value to the president. The proportion of offices he may fill in the executive branch has diminished greatly since the days of the Jacksonian spoils system. Under the Pendleton Act of 1883, as amended periodically, more and more federal positions have been brought into the competitive civil service. They are filled by examination and protected from political influence by rules against partisan activity and arbitrary dismissal. Of the fraction remaining within the president's power of appointment, and of federal judgeships, all of which are his to fill, a good many are actually controlled by the Senate under the custom of senatorial courtesy. The few appointments left, such as members of the cabinet, their assistants, and the assistants' assistants, then must be made from among those who are both capable and available, a select and homogeneous group. Typically they are well-educated urbanites with experience in government. The differences in the qualities of appointees to these positions are nearly as great from department to department as from one administration to another. Catholics have been attracted to the Justice Department, traditionally; Episcopalians to State and Defense; and members of farm interest groups to Agriculture; but there were as many members of Phi Beta Kappa in the Eisenhower administration as in President Kennedy's, and only slightly fewer than average with government experience in President Eisenhower's de-spite the dry years for Republicans from 1933 to 1953.[3] The patterns of appointment suggest that the president's impact on the executive may be blunted by informal as well as by formal constraints on White House recruiting. Lastly, when he does make a satisfying appointment, it may sour. In the words of the old complaint, "Every time I fill a vacant place I make a hundred malcontents and one ingrate."

The president faces similar formal and informal constraints on his power of removal. Since the Constitution is silent on the question of the president's powers in this area, there has been room for experimenta-tion by the three branches. The main arguments have been that the removal power is inherently executive, except for impeachment and conviction of high crimes and misdemeanors by Congress; that it is a part of the power to appoint shared by the president and the Senate; and that it is subject to regulation by Congress through ordinary legis-lation.[4] The first Congress decided in a close vote that the president had the authority to remove officials appointed with the advice and consent of the Senate, but the debate remained alive. In 1867 Congress changed position, passing a Tenure of Office Act which required the president to obtain Senate permission for the removal of any official appointed with its advice and consent, a measure aimed squarely at Andrew Johnson.[5] President Johnson's refusal to obey the act was the central complaint in his impeachment and near conviction. The act was weak-ened by Congress during the administration of Ulysses S. Grant and repealed in 1887.[6]

The Supreme Court at last settled the question in 1926 in favor of the president. It overturned an act of Congress of 1876 patterned after the Tenure of Office Act, and it condemned the latter in passing, retrospec-tively, as an invasion of the president's exclusive power to remove executive officers whom he has appointed with the advice and consent of the Senate.[7] The question was whether or not Woodrow Wilson might lawfully remove a postmaster in Oregon without the advice and consent of the Senate required by the act. A former president, now chief justice, William Howard Taft, in an opinion uniting law, history, and personal experience, transcended the problems of the post office to argue an interpretation of the Constitution allowing the president full control of his appointees.

> Made responsible under the Constitution for the effective enforcement of the law, the president needs as an indispensable aid to meet it the disciplinary influence upon those who act under him of a reserve power of removal. . . .
>
> He must place in each member of his official family, and his chief executive subordinates, implicit faith. The moment that he loses confidence in the intelligence, ability, judgment or loyalty of any one of them, he must have the power to remove him without delay. To require him to file charges and submit them to the consideration of the Senate might make impossible that unity and coordination in executive administration essential to effective action. . . .
>
> The power to remove inferior executive officers, like that to remove superior executive officers, is an incident of the power to appoint them, and is in its nature an executive power.[8]

Although the president's power to remove executive officials confirmed by the Senate has been limited in other ways since, the Court's exclusion of the Senate from the removal process has held firm. Of course the great mass of federal positions filled competitively by examination are beyond the president's removal power. An ordinary civil servant is removable for reasons, and by a process, provided by statute.

The other formal means of controlling executive programs, used by the president in concert with his powers of supervision, appointment, and dismissal, are the clearance powers administered by the Office of Management and Budget, created as the Bureau of the Budget in 1921 and moved from the Treasury Department into the Executive Office of the President in 1939. Acting for the president, the OMB approves, disapproves, or amends requests for money and new authority directed to Congress by agencies of the executive branch. In theory the powers of budgetary and legislative clearance give the president control of the programs of that branch, subject to the will of Congress. In practice the influence they afford the president is as marginal as his power over personnel.

Each year the OMB considers the budget requests of executive agencies in the light of the president's policy preferences—"the program of the president"—and its own assessments of the efficiency and effectiveness of the agencies' performance in the past. Congress may ignore the president's wishes by appropriating less than the OMB requests, or by appropriating more, in the past a much rarer occurrence. Traditionally the president and the OMB have been little more inclined than Congress to make large adjustments from one year to the next. They have considered it simpler and safer to continue established programs more or less intact. In the beginning of his second term, with the confidence that goes with a landslide reelection (or the sang-froid of one who is ineligible for reelection), President Nixon made drastic inroads upon domestic programs, asking less of Congress, vetoing appropriations, impounding funds, and abolishing programs by executive fiat. But his behavior was exceptional. Most presidents have found it more profitable to sustain domestic projects than to stir up antagonism inside and outside of government by cutting costs.

The president's requests are by no means final. Still, given the tendency of Congress to reduce the figures it receives from the executive branch, it might be supposed that his power to punish agencies by cutting their requests beforehand is substantial. In reality the president and the OMB are little more inclined than Congress to make large adjustments in the sums requested. The political risks of disrupting existing allocations of resources are too great. It is safer and simpler to continue established programs with marginal adjustments. The current budget remains a good predictor of the next year's figures.

The legislative clearance function of the OMB has kept pace with the aspirations of the White House over the years, growing from a routine money-saving device into a broad instrument of executive management. In the 1920s, economy-minded presidents regarded legislative clearance as a part of the budget process—a way to hold down the costs of government. Franklin Roosevelt channeled proposals, irrespective of budgetary implications, through the clearance system as an anticipatory exercise of the presidential veto power. He gave the legislative clearance staff responsibility for recommending signature or veto of measures passed by Congress. Beginning with Harry Truman the staff acquired the further task of initiating and developing presidential legislative proposals, with the assistance of the agencies.[9] In short, as the presidency became more positive than negative, so did legislative clearance. The executive can now speak to Congress with one voice and present its legislative program systematically. Like the budget itself, however, legislative clearance is a presidential power exercised within the political constraints of a legislative system which is conservative in operation.

A common assumption in and about the White House is that a president can centralize the marketing of decisions and the monitoring of compliance by using the several tools of management together. There have been two general strategies for perfecting centralization and for assuring presidential control of the executive branch. One is characteristic of Republican presidents, the other of Democratic presidents. Neither works in any sustained way, because in normal times political influence over domestic programs is too well dispersed in the political system to be gathered back by administrative devices; but the effort is made.

The Republican strategy, favored by Presidents Dwight Eisenhower and Richard Nixon, is to bring order to the complexities of domestic administration with a well-organized presidential bureaucracy to make policy recommendations to the president and to coordinate the activities of the operating agencies. The people around the president have well-defined functions and ranks—the horizontal and vertical dimensions of an organized chart. They form several organizational layers, with few overlapping assignments. Few people report to the president.

Dwight Eisenhower enlarged the president's staff and formalized its work, placing at its apex the assistant to the president, Sherman Adams, a gate-keeper who decided what and whom the president would see. Because it was President Eisenhower's wish not to be encumbered with unnecessary detail, Adams filtered out all but a trickle of people and papers, a duty which did not endear him to the Washington community. And because Eisenhower wanted important issues to be presented succinctly, accompanied by recommendations for presidential action, Adams had to be an exacting master of the presidential staff. To Adams, his staff, and the cabinet, President Eisenhower delegated authority generously in domestic affairs, particularly when he was preoccupied with problems of peace.

President Nixon reorganized and further enlarged and formalized the presidential staff, creating a Domestic Council as a counterpart of the National Security Council and a new budget agency to supervise the administration of policy formulated in the two councils and approved by the president.

On the model of the National Security Council, which included the president, the vice-president, and cabinet members from the two departments most involved in foreign affairs, State and Defense, the Domestic Council consisted of the president, the vice-president, and appropriate members of the cabinet. Its purpose, according to President Nixon's message to Congress, was to make policy proposals to the president, defining goals, assessing national needs, reviewing present policy, and recommending changes.[10] The assistant to the president for domestic affairs, John Ehrlichman, was given responsibilities and staff similar to Henry Kissinger's in national security affairs.

The new Office of Management and Budget was to have, in addition to the budgetary, legislative, and management-consultant functions of its predecessor, the more active duties of overseeing the administration of presidential policies, coordinating the work of related agencies, evaluating their performance, and suggesting administrative reforms.

The implication of President Nixon's first reorganization was that in domestic affairs administrative routine would be the continuing responsibility of cabinet members and other agency heads individually, but that departures from the routine would be proposed by the Domestic Council and the OMB in matters of policy and administration—ends and means—respectively.

As in the Eisenhower years there were varying views of the efficacy of such management reforms. Cabinet members, always in some doubt as to their status in the administration, had reason to feel still more estranged.[11] Skeptics on the outside viewed the reforms as an attempt to cure the ills of bureaucracy with more bureaucracy. The president saw the enlargement of staff and formalization of procedures as a way of tightening controls and of filtering out unimportant matters for decision at lower levels in order to free the president for important ones. He felt the division of labor between policy-making and administration, and between foreign and domestic affairs, was practicable. In his second term he instituted new reforms which added still another level of organization, a domestic super-cabinet of three, between the White House and the operating departments. Soon, however, the Watergate revelations forced his most trusted aides from office and checked the drift toward centralization of power within the executive branch.

Most Democratic presidents have favored a White House bureaucracy as simple and as small as possible. When he took office, John Kennedy dismantled most of President Eisenhower's machinery for making and implementing decisions, on the theory derived from the experience of Franklin Roosevelt that an overblown staff diminishes the power of the president. Like Roosevelt, Kennedy wished to be accessible to his assistants—in Roosevelt's administration, indeed, nearly a hundred people inside and outside the White House were privileged to telephone the president without giving reasons to a secretary.[12] The fewer organizational filters the better, in the opinion of both men.

The Democratic tendency is the opposite of the Republican in all key respects: in administrative jargon, a "flat" organization with a minimum of intermediaries, rather than a tall hierarchical structure; and shifting, overlapping assignments to subordinates in place of a careful division of labor. The hope is to prevent White House bureaucrats from becoming overprotective of the president or proprietary. It was Roosevelt's practice, followed in varying degrees by John Kennedy and Lyndon Johnson, to set two people to similar tasks, not informing them of the duplication, in order to rise above the limitations of each. Their preference for competitive check-and-balance administration was unsettling to the subordinates, needless to say.

The most obvious lesson to be drawn from the cyclical imposition of ordered hierarchy and disordered competitiveness in the White House as parties succeed one another is that no one has yet devised an unassailable plan of management. The problem remains of assuring the president information from below to make policy decisions and effective control of the bureaucracy once his decisions are made. On the policy side, however, there would seem to be some merit in the ordered competitiveness of multiple advocacy, a proposal to institutionalize and regulate policy conflict inside the executive branch, drawn eclectically from the successes and lessons of failure of recent administrations. Under this plan presidents would assign responsibility for the maintenance of a number of centers of policy analysis and enjoy more balanced advice and intelligence from the executive hierarchy than the monolithic or the haphazardly pluralistic system offers.[13]

Under the Constitution the president enjoys a degree of loosely defined executive power, as we have noted, and the authority to appoint key officials—subject to Senate confirmation in most cases—and to remove them. By law he has powers of budgetary and legislative clearance with which to reward, punish, and coordinate the agencies of the executive branch. And he is at liberty to rearrange the structure and functions of his administrative staff to bring the White House and the agencies of the executive branch together. Yet for all his formal authority, the president has little to offer the people in these agencies in exchange for loyalty. To the extent that they engage in profitable transactions with legislators and favored constituents, bureaucrats are disinclined to serve the president's interests. The norm is a modest level of routine interaction.

There have been exceptions to the rule of lukewarm bureaucratic relations, however: periods of warm exchange and frigid uncooperativeness.

Abnormal Cooperation with Bureaucrats in Civilian Programs

Subordinates in civilian programs who have engaged in intense exchanges with the president have been for the most part newcomers to government. Andrew Jackson and Abraham Lincoln had close relations with the bureaucracy as patronage presidents, hiring great numbers of new people. Both believed that the work of dispensing jobs, however onerous and time-consuming, was vital to presidential leadership. They traded jobs for loyalty—Lincoln especially did so in the turmoil of civil war. After the inauguration of a competitive civil service had reduced the patronage power of the White House, this kind of exchange was to be found mainly in newly organized or reorganized agencies. A new agency, with a combination of new people and transfers from existing agencies, is valuable to a president because it is flexible and tractable. A new agency is ready to exchange because, without an experienced clientele at home or on Capitol Hill, it needs presidential support and protection to survive.

During the New Deal, Roosevelt and Congress created many new agencies rather than entrust new programs to old agencies. The new agencies reported directly to the president and held his loyalty and attention. The early welfare programs are a case in point. Roosevelt directed the establishment of one after another, both to meet new needs and to compete with one another experimentally: the Federal Emergency Relief Administration, to provide immediate, direct relief; the Civil Works Administration, to experiment in work relief, a more costly but more humane program; the Works Progress Administration, to employ unskilled labor in projects of modest size (all three of these agencies were administered by Harry Hopkins); the Public Works Administration, to try out a program of larger construction projects under the direction of Harold Ickes; and the Federal Surplus Relief Corporation, to distribute food to the unemployed. They fought for funds, personnel, and the favor of the president. When one of the programs had outlived its usefulness, because a better way of taking care of needy people had been devised or because of public criticism, it was disbanded.[14]

Roosevelt's method was to watch and wait while his associates tested their ideas in new programs. He was a pragmatist for whom policymaking and administration were inseparable; he trusted tangible experience more than principles or predictions when he had to make a policy decision. His reluctance to commit himself without the luxury of a period of trial and error was akin to the traditional refusal of federal courts to hand down premature opinions on the constitutionality of legislation, in part because the impact of legislation—its costs and benefits—cannot be known until the bare words have been translated into the actions and reactions of real people.

In a broad sense the New Deal was a time of testing from beginning to end. The common themes of the early programs were government and business cooperation and social and economic planning. Where these experiments were to lead could not be foretold—perhaps to an abandonment of the capitalist economy. But within a few years the programs changed course, or were replaced by more conservative ones regulating or subsidizing existing institutions. The transformation of the Tennessee Valley Authority from a multipurpose project for reclamation and economic development with overtones of utopian social experimentation into a businesslike producer of electrical power illustrates the trend. Advisors and administrators as well as programs were replaced as Roosevelt felt his way along.

After the New Deal, presidents devoted themselves to newly organized or reorganized programs less often. But when they wanted to lend a program their support, a favorite expedient was to place it close to the White House on the federal organization chart. In 1958, as a symbol of the government's determination to compete with the Soviet Union in space, not only was a new agency created, the National Aeronautics and Space Administration, but a National Aeronautics and Space Council was established in the Executive Office of the President, composed of the vice-president as chairman and the secretaries of defense and state, the chairman of the Atomic Energy Commission, and the administrator of NASA.

Similarly, the Office of Economic Opportunity was placed in the Executive Office of the President at its inception in 1964 as a mark of its importance to President Johnson. The Jacksonian quality of the "war on poverty"—the president as tribune of the masses, the poor enlisted in local policy-making and administration—gave it a political appeal that behooved the president to keep the OEO in the White House orbit.

President Nixon obtained legislation from Congress to reorganize the government's cancer research effort and render it directly responsible to the White House. In his 1971 State of the Union message, he said, "The time has come when the same kind of concentrated effort that split the atom and took man to the moon should be turned toward conquering this dread disease."[15] The controversial reorganization gave the president the power to appoint the director of the National Cancer Institute, eighteen members of a national cancer advisory board, and the three members of a president's cancer panel whose duty it was to monitor the cancer program, meet at least monthly, and report to the president on progress in the search for a cure.[16] If and when the Cancer Institute found a cure, the reorganization promised the president the opportunity to announce the good tidings to the world.

In each case—relief, space, poverty, and cancer—the rapid promotion of a program of political value to the president was undertaken through a new or reorganized agency with special ties to the White House. From the viewpoint of a new agency, White House protection is an asset in its competition for funds and authority. By contrast, the typical established agency with friends and supporters in Congress and the constituencies has no need for White House favor, which is impermanent.

Abnormal Uncooperativeness with Bureaucrats in Civilian Programs

At the other extreme are a good many instances of presidents or bureaucrats refusing to engage in exchange because of self-interest or principle. John Kennedy ignored the Department of State on important occasions. He was more trustful of McGeorge Bundy, his assistant for national security affairs, than he was of Secretary of State Dean Rusk and the bureaucracy at Foggy Bottom. "The President used to divert himself with the dream of establishing a secret office of thirty people or so to run foreign policy while maintaining the State Department as a facade in which people might contentedly carry papers from bureau to bureau."[17] This was a good forecast, in fact, of things to come. The transfer of power was completed under Henry Kissinger, before his appointment as secretary of state. The prestige of the State Department fell as low as it had in the dark days when Joseph McCarthy used the foreign service as a general purpose scapegoat for problems of the nation and the world. It was illustrative of its reduced state that the department did not know of President Nixon's impending trip to Moscow in 1972. Perhaps a few senior officials were aware of White House plans; others, to their humiliation, were informed shortly before the public announcement by a routine memorandum from the FBI, which had obtained its information from undercover contacts in the American Communist party.[18]

The State Department had declined because of the conformist tendencies of the foreign service; the increasing need for specialists in science, economics, agriculture, and other disciplines rather than for gentleman generalists in international programs; the greater secrecy and flexibility of decision-making in the White House; and the personal interest of recent presidents in firsthand direction of foreign affairs.[19] When a department offers the president less than he needs, he turns to others to fill the gaps.

And it works the other way around: if orders from above violate the demands of conscience, bureaucrats may refuse to transact. Normally the refusal is covert—sabotage, for example, or leaks to the press to bring the orders into disrepute—but in the early months of the Nixon administration there were cases of open, organized opposition of civil servants to White House policy. In late 1969, sixty-five civil rights lawyers in the Department of Justice signed a statement protesting the administration's school desegregation policy. Members of the group who declined to go into court seeking desegregation delays resigned or were dismissed.[20]

In the Department of Health, Education, and Welfare a few months later some 2,000 civil servants, predominantly executives and professionals, signed a petition calling for the secretary to defend the department's weakening position on civil rights. Concurrently about 125 of the department's specialists in civil rights wrote the president to protest the removal of the head of their office and to ask for clarification of the administration's intentions. HEW Secretary Robert Finch scheduled a meeting with several hundred members of the department in the headquarters auditorium, to be carried by television to HEW cafeterias throughout the city, in order to discuss the issues and questions of his leadership, but at the eleventh hour he entered a hospital with a nervous condition. His remarks, read by a subordinate, were booed and hissed.[21]

At about the same time in the Department of State about 250 employees sent a letter to Secretary William Rogers criticizing American military involvement in Cambodia. The letter expressed "concern and apprehension over the enlargement of hostilities in Southeast Asia" and asked the secretary to "seek reconsideration" of the underlying policy.[22]

James Reston of the *Times* commented, "The new thing here is the extent of the revolt at HEW and at the State Department against the policies and priorities of the administration. Like the students, the civil servants are protesting against being taken for granted and this could have a profound effect on the future of the American government."[23] Hindsight suggested otherwise. There was no evidence that the outbreaks affected administration policy. In the few domestic programs in which a president takes a close interest there may well be division and discontent—the same might occur in, say, the Department of Agriculture if a chief executive experimented with new farm policies—but the White House is free to ignore bureaucratic dissent or to stifle it.

A year later there was some discord among members of the Volunteers in Service to America, also known as the domestic peace corps, during a conference of the National VISTA Alliance, an organization of members and former members. Approximately 400 men and women in attendance voted unanimously to recommend that Richard Nixon "be sentenced to being dumped as president of the United States and that sentencing should be carried out by political education in the communities in which VISTAs work." The president was described as "an active enemy of the poor and underemployed and unemployed."[24] As in the case of civil rights activists within the executive branch, these VISTA employees demonstrated an unwillingness to engage in transactions with a president who represented an ideological break with previous administrations.

There is one kind of agency in which the right of disagreement with the president is honored by a special form of organization, and that is the independent regulatory commission. Beginning in 1887 with the Interstate Commerce Commission, Congress has from time to time created agencies with mixed administrative, legislative, and judicial functions to regulate special segments of the economy without White House direction. They are governed by boards appointed within narrow statutory limits by the president. Typically terms are fixed and staggered, there may be no more than a bare majority of any one party, and removal must be for reasons set out in the law, such as "inefficiency, neglect of duty, and malfeasance in office."

The rule of *Myers* v. *United States,*[25] that the president may remove his appointees at will, was amended in the case of *Humphrey's Executor* v. *United States* in 1935 to sanction this form of agency. Humphrey, a member of the Federal Trade Commission reappointed to a seven-year term by President Hoover in 1931, was asked to resign by President Roosevelt in 1933 on grounds "that the aims and purposes of the administration with respect to the work of the commission can be carried out most effectively with personnel of my own selection." Humphrey refused and was removed summarily by the president.[26] In deciding against the president, the Court held that Congress might establish an independent commission which could not "in any proper sense be characterized as an arm or an eye of the executive. Its duties are performed without executive leave and, in the contemplation of the statute, must be free from executive control."[27] The Supreme Court is so confident of the propriety of circumscribing the president's removal power that it has extended the Humphrey doctrine to an agency with adjudicatory functions, the War Claims Commission, for which Congress prescribed no limitations on removal at all.[28]

Subjects now insulated from the president in this manner include the regulation of stock exchanges, electric power production, railroad and airline rates, telephone rates, radio and television broadcasting, labor relations, and honesty in advertising. In each instance the president gains a measure of influence by making annual appointments until, with good fortune, he has named a majority of the board, vacancy by vacancy, in the same way that he may hope to appoint a Supreme Court of his own. But in the commissions, as on the Court, a degree of independent mindedness is to be expected. If they disagree with the president there is very little he can do. Presidential advisors have thought of reorganizing the commissions under the hegemony of the White House —the proposals of former Securities and Exchange Commission Chairman James Landis to John Kennedy, for example—but Congress shows no interest.

The commissioners themselves are content both with their independence of the White House and their productive exchanges with Congress and the industries they regulate. To them the interest and concern on the part of members of the White House may represent less a promise of support than a threat of favor-seeking or empire-building by people using the White House for personal advancement.[29]

Even agencies under the nominal control of the president, whose top officials are freely removable, frequently exhibit an independence and unwillingness to exchange that is characteristic of the regulatory commissions. Patterns of influence in the domestic policy-making system often bypass the executive and the other agents of the majority will, despite appearances. The president's interactions with the bureaucracy in civilian programs, in sum, tend to be limited in number and intensity.

Traditional Relations with Bureaucrats in Military Programs

The relations of the White House and the civilian and military bureaucrats in military programs changed in the 1960s and 1970s. A new norm replaced the old. Through 1960, the final year of the Eisenhower administration, the pattern of interaction was one of antagonism rather than exchange. On balance, each side coerced the other without expectation of mutual gain. The interaction was generally viewed as a constitutional problem of civilian control of the military. The framers of the Constitution had believed that civilian control would be secured by the citizen-soldiers of the armed forces: men taking up arms in time of crisis, tempering any militaristic tendencies in their units, and returning to civilian life at the end of hostilities. With the rise of a professional military corps, however, civilian control hinged uneasily on the ability of political leaders to direct the military and on the willingness of the military to abstain from politics. Enjoying many points of access for pressure politics—national and state, executive and legislative—the military and its allies sometimes competed politically for power and money along with businessmen, farmers, and the rest of the country's citizens.[30]

The removal of disobedient military commanders—the unmovable McClellan from command of the Army of the Potomac by Abraham Lincoln in 1862 or the unmanageable MacArthur from command of United Nations forces in Korea and United States forces in the Far East by Harry Truman in 1951—was the last spectacular resort of presidents bent on maintaining civilian supremacy. In the MacArthur confrontation it was a brilliant, egotistical, theatrically heroic general versus a former captain of artillery and haberdasher in the White House who was under political attack from all sides and near bottom in the opinion polls. General MacArthur, with his contempt for the president imperfectly concealed, made a number of policy statements to the press which were at odds with the program of the administration.[31] The last straw was his reply to a message from Joseph W. Martin, the Republican minority leader of the House of Representatives. Martin had proposed the use of Nationalist Chinese troops in the war and asked for the general's own views. MacArthur responded:

My views and recommendations with respect to the situation created by Red China's entry into war against us in Korea have been submitted to Washington in most complete detail. Generally these views are well known and clearly understood, as they follow the conventional pattern of meeting force with maximum counterforce as we have never failed to do in the past. Your view with respect to the utilization of the Chinese forces on Formosa is in conflict with neither logic nor this tradition.

It seems strangely difficult for some to realize that here in Asia is where the communist conspirators have elected to make their play for global conquest, and that we have joined the issue thus raised on the battlefield; that here we fight Europe's wars with arms while the diplomats there still fight it with words; that if we lose the war to communism in Asia the fall of Europe is inevitable, win it and Europe most probably would avoid war and yet preserve freedom. As you point out, we must win. There is no substitute for victory.[32]

The letter was made public and created an international stir, as MacArthur might have anticipated. He was relieved of his command forthwith.

It was another hero-general, Dwight Eisenhower, who restated the old problem of civilian control in all of its modern complexity, however. He reminded the country that military disobedience was not its only manifestation. In his farewell address he warned the American people of "a permanent armaments industry of vast proportions."

This conjunction of an immense military establishment and a large arms industry is new in American experience. The total influence—economic, political, even spiritual—is felt in every city, every state house, every office of the federal government. We recognize the imperative need for this development. Yet we must not fail to comprehend its grave implications. Our toil, resources, and livelihood are all involved; so is the very structure of our society.

In the councils of government, we must guard against the acquisition of unwarranted influence, whether sought or unsought, by the military-industrial complex. The potential for the disastrous rise of misplaced power exists and will persist. We must never let the weight of this combination endanger our liberties or democratic processes. We should take nothing for granted. Only an alert and knowledgeable citizenry can compel the proper meshing of the huge industrial and military machinery of defense with our peaceful methods and goals, so that security and liberty may prosper together.[33]

Despite his life as a professional soldier, perhaps because of it, President Eisenhower was a champion of the tradition of military subordination to civilian political leadership.

The McNamara Years— A Transition

The administrations of John Kennedy and Lyndon Johnson were years of inconsistency in the relations of the White House and the Pentagon. On the one hand they represented the most deliberate, systematic effort in the nation's history to bring the military under civilian control, and on the other they fostered a growing mutuality of interest in a strong, active military machine. Added to the traditional antagonism and coercive imposition of civilian values on the military there was a new willingness to engage in exchanges. The contrary tendencies in policy matched the ambivalence in the attitudes of the two presidents toward military power. Students of the period find support for widely divergent theories of presidential intentions.

The battle for civilian supremacy was centered in the office of the secretary of defense, specifically in the budgetary innovations of Robert McNamara. Brought to Washington from the presidency of the Ford Motor Company, where he was known as a tough, intellectual manager, McNamara soon displayed a style of his own in an administration resplendent with style. He was brusque and businesslike with august generals and admirals, and he exhibited such command of the details of Pentagon business that he could win arguments with senior men in the bureaucracy and the committees of Congress. All in all he was very unlike the insouciant "Engine Charlie" Wilson, former president of General Motors, who served as Eisenhower's secretary of defense and displayed the same tenuous control of the armed services that President Eisenhower exercised over the executive branch as a whole.

More important than style, however, was Secretary McNamara's introduction of PPBS—the planning-programming-budgeting system developed by Rand Corporation consultants to the air force—for the management of his department. Conventional budgeting, the annual process of securing funds for each unit and subunit of the government, had come under increasing criticism for its failure to provide an analysis of expenditures by function. Unenlightened allocations of resources were made from a budget document showing only that an agency or a bureau wanted so much more or less this year than last. Managers and legislators who were content with a superficial account of an agency's business, whose motives, perhaps, were simply to hold expenditures down, had all the information they needed. But the advantage of PPBS was, simply, that it offered the secretary, the president, and inquisitive congressmen a picture of the *work* of the department in addition to the cost of running each component. Because the civilians of the 1960s were more informed than their predecessors, they were more influential.

Under the new system, the outputs of the department—the "capabilities"—were gathered into a number of programs, such as "strategic retaliatory forces," "continental air and missile defense forces," and "airlift and sealift." Contributions of the army, navy, and air force were blended freely in a departure from the service-by-service and unit-by-unit analysis of outputs in the past. While the services remained separate for housekeeping purposes, each with its own hierarchy, uniforms, and traditions, they were expected to integrate functionally. With costs determined for each program, the government for the first time could plot military expenditures by function.

Furthermore in planning future expenditures Secretary McNamara could use this information system to minimize costs for a given level of output (or to maximize output for a given level of expenditure) by comparing alternative means to the ends contemplated in each program—for example, the cost-benefit analysis, so-called, of land-based missiles versus submarine-based missiles versus bombers carrying atomic weapons as alternative "strategic retaliatory forces."

As anticipated, PPBS had a profound impact on the way the Pentagon was run. Decisions once the responsibility of the separate services now were made in the office of the secretary of defense, which acquired new staff and computers for the task. Budgeting grew from a periodic process of soliciting funds into a full-time management system, with annual estimates for Congress an adjunct. Budgeting, management, and policy-making became inseparable. And with the massive systematization of input and output data for the defense establishment in PPBS, projections of future defense needs, force levels, and costs years into the future were feasible for the first time.

But all of the sophistication of planning, programming, and budgeting could not prevent errors of judgment in defense policy-making in the Kennedy and Johnson administrations. As one of a growing number of critics noted, with some justice, McNamara made no small mistakes. In 1964 he assured the nation that American soldiers would be home from Vietnam by Christmas of 1965. Stressing weaponry in his computations, he consistently underestimated the fighting ability of the guerillas his forces faced in Vietnam. Even in the case of weapons systems, he underestimated costs and overestimated benefits—his swing-wing tactical fighter aircraft, the TFX, later named the F-111, was meant to serve the needs of both the air force and the navy economically and efficiently. Instead, over many years, the F-111 was buffeted by interservice rivalry, technical failures, and cost overruns.[34] McNamara's efforts to build an electronic barrier between North and South Vietnam failed.

PPBS coordinated and rationalized the components of the vast American military machine, eliminating some of the duplication and waste endemic in the military, and established an independent standard for evaluating proposals of the three service bureaucracies. What it could not do, of course, was to guarantee that the information fed into the computers concerning the identity, strength, and intentions of adversaries and the projected cost and effectiveness of new American weapons systems was sound. What seemed authoritative at the time, expounded by a forceful secretary of defense, now looks like simple dogmatism. The skeptics who had preferred the safety-in-numbers of fragmented decision-making all along and who had questioned the feasibility of separating ends from means in government returned to favor in Washington.[35]

McNamara's "revolution" was the ambitious effort of a civilian secretary to wrest military policy-making from the military. Whatever its imperfections, it centralized decision-making and altered the balance of power between the political leaders of the country and the bureaucracy in military programs. The acquiescence of military bureaucrats in the reforms can only be explained by the overriding interest of both sides in military expansion in the 1960s. President Kennedy entered office with a commitment to build up American military forces of all kinds, from missiles to counterinsurgents; in office he initiated the escalation of American military force in Vietnam. President Johnson continued in the same direction. Every year but one in these two administrations the defense budget grew substantially. In exchange terms the military acquiesced because they were content to trade autonomy for growth, a state of mind paralleling that of American industry, described by Galbraith as preferring growth to profit.[36]

After McNamara—
A New Norm

The internal contradiction of the McNamara period—a strong assertion of civilian control with the military getting most of what it could hope for—gave way to a more straightforward deference to military values in the Nixon administration.

President Nixon's first secretary of defense, Melvin Laird, discarded most of McNamara's innovations. In the first months of the administration the choice of alternatives within major programs was restored to the separate services, subject of course to the approval of the secretary and the president, and the PPBS revolution was over, mourned neither by conservatives nor by liberals.[37]

In policy as in procedures the military bureaucracy had reason to feel more comfortable in the Nixon administration. Even more than his predecessors, President Nixon stressed military strength as a basis for negotiating and keeping the peace. In the 1972 presidential campaign, the difference between his policy of military preparedness and Senator McGovern's promise of a reduction of defense spending was the clearest of all before the electorate. While President Nixon sometimes overruled the concerted advice of the military bureaucracy—notably in the withdrawal of ground forces from Vietnam, the destruction of stockpiled biological weapons, and the intense bombing of Hanoi late in 1972 —more often than not he followed it. He pressed for military pay increases while fighting inflation in other segments of the labor force. The Pentagon enjoyed in Richard Nixon a president who valued military power.

In the 1970s the military became more the ally of the White House than its competitor. Suspicion gave way to understanding. One need not seek an explanation of the new relationship in a theory of military conspiracy. It is enough to note that presidents—and some far more than others—value the psychological and political fruits of a large, prospering military machine.

Most presidents are buoyed psychologically by actual or vicarious participation in military maneuvers, perhaps as an adult version of the child's delight in bathtub fleets and backyard rocketry. Certainly the grandeur and responsiveness of the military in action are a pleasing contrast to the remoteness and intractability of other components of the executive branch. Of the modern presidents, only Dwight Eisenhower, the general, was free of the armada complex—the others were tempted by ships, planes, and other instruments of war. Franklin Roosevelt and John Kennedy preferred ships, Lyndon Johnson planes, but the sentiment was the same. There was in each of them a measure of Theodore Roosevelt, big game hunter and eternal boy, who compensated for a boyhood of sickness, frailty, and myopia with a rugged adult life of military adventure and derring-do.

In addition, a president is assured a decent show of cordiality and deference from the military, a welcome relief from the rigors of interaction with the Senate or the press. During Lyndon Johnson's administration, when the president was the prime target of antiwar protesters, the Secret Service feared violence in public confrontations. Military bases at home and abroad were nearly the only strongholds where he could enjoy friendly faces and the cheers of the throng. When President Nixon broke his Watergate seclusion, it was to speak on military affairs to military families on a moored aircraft carrier.

Richard Nixon's closest identification was with the space program. He thrilled at the launching of rockets to the moon. He wore an astronaut's jacket in moments of relaxation, the equivalent of Theodore Roosevelt's six-shooters and cowboy hat or Winston Churchill's naval blues. Once he traveled five thousand miles unannounced to the Pacific to welcome three astronauts from space.[38] Like Lyndon Johnson, he found emotional release in flying.

The evidence is that even if he did not regard it as an important instrument of national policy, the typical president would value military force as an extension of his own personality. It is hard to know, contemplating Theodore Roosevelt's confession that he would "welcome almost any war" because "this country needs one," where personality ends and public policy begins.[39] Today Theodore Roosevelt would be called a warmonger. Military activity is justified not for its own sake now, but as a means to a higher end on the order of national honor, protection of American lives, freedom, and world peace. Still, there are echoes of Theodore Roosevelt in the rhetoric of a gentler man, John Kennedy, that marks the break with the relative quiet of the Eisenhower years. It is instructive to recall the tone of Kennedy's inaugural address:

> Let every nation know, whether it wishes us well or ill, that we shall pay any price, bear any burden, meet any hardship, support any friend, oppose any foe, in order to assure the survival and the success of liberty. . . .

To those peoples in the huts and villages of half the globe struggling to break the bonds of mass misery, we pledge our best efforts to help them help themselves, for whatever period is required. . . .

Now the trumpet summons us again—not as a call to bear arms, though arms we need; not as a call to battle, though embattled we are; but a call to bear the burden of a long twilight struggle, year in, and year out, "rejoicing in hope, patient in tribulation"—a struggle against the common enemies of man: tyranny, poverty, disease, and war itself. . . .

In the long history of the world, only a few generations have been granted the role of defending freedom in its hour of maximum danger. I do not shrink from this responsibility—I welcome it.[40]

As the Pentagon Papers revealed, war was a vital instrument of national policy in the 1960s. Presidents Kennedy and Johnson were not, on the whole, victims of bad advice and bad intelligence, although their advice and intelligence was often bad. They *chose* war in Vietnam, but defended their decisions with less and less candor as the years went by. In the Nixon administration the ambivalence evaporated. It became clear, at first more from deeds than from words, that the threat of military force was the core of American foreign policy. Much of the duplicity of the 1960s, such as winning "the hearts and minds" of the people of Vietnam, was abandoned.

The domestic uses of the military also gained importance in the Nixon administration. Franklin Roosevelt had set a precedent in approving the relocation of the Japanese-Americans from the West Coast in World War II, a policy conceived and executed by the military. Hesitantly in the 1960s and boldly in the 1970s, attorneys general and presidents used the armed forces for control of civil disorders and for surveillance of civilian political activity. The Central Intelligence Agency began training municipal police in political intelligence-gathering despite a clear statutory prohibition of such activity.[41] In 1972 a divided Supreme Court upheld the president by rejecting a challenge, based upon the freedoms of the First Amendment, to the use of the military personnel for domestic surveillance.[42] In 1973 Central Intelligence Agency personnel were discovered to have been involved in the political scandals associated with the Watergate break-in. When his right-hand man, H. R. Haldeman, was forced from office in the wake of Watergate, President Nixon named a general as an apolitical replacement, as President Eisenhower had done in similar circumstances years before. The increasing level of exchange between the White House and the Pentagon in domestic affairs reflected a feeling that the military bureaucracy was more attuned to presidential interests than the civilian bureaucracy was, and more reliable.

In the past the effect of this feeling was a turning of White House attention from domestic to foreign and military programs, rather than the application of military force to domestic problems. In the 1970s the military showed first signs of becoming a versatile instrument of government at home as well as abroad.

Notes

[1] *Opinions of the Attorney General,* 624, 625–26 (1823).

[2] James D. Richardson, ed., *Messages and Papers of the Presidents* (Washington, D.C.: Government Printing Office, 1896), Vol. 3, 79.

[3] Dean E. Mann, "The Selection of Federal Executives," *American Political Science Review,* LVIII, No. 1 (1964), 81–99.

[4] Leonard D. White, *The Federalists* (New York: The Macmillan Company, 1948), pp. 20–21.

[5] 14 Stat. 430 (1867).

[6] 24 Stat. 500 (1887).

[7] *Myers* v. *United States,* 272 U.S. 52 (1926).

[8] *Ibid.,* 132, 134, 161.

[9] Richard E. Neustadt, "Presidency and Legislation: The Growth of Central Clearance," *American Political Science Review,* XLVIII, No. 3 (1954), 641–71.

[10] *New York Times,* March 13, 1970, p. 18.

[11] *New York Times,* March 13, 1970, p. 18; June 11, 1970, p. 37; June 12, 1970, p. 20; June 15, 1970, p. 42.

[12] Arthur M. Schlesinger, Jr., *The Coming of the New Deal* (Boston: Houghton Mifflin Company, 1958), pp. 520–32.

[13] Alexander L. George, "The Case for Multiple Advocacy in Making Foreign Policy," *American Political Science Review,* LXVI, No. 3 (1972), 751–85.

[14] Arthur M. Schlesinger, Jr., *The Politics of Upheaval* (Boston: Houghton Mifflin Company, 1960), pp. 264–70, 343–61.

[15] *Congressional Quarterly Almanac* (1971), p. 557.

[16] 85 Stat. 78 (1971).

[17] Arthur M. Schlesinger, Jr., *A Thousand Days* (Boston: Houghton Mifflin Company, 1965), p. 413.

[18] *New York Times,* November 22, 1971, p. 15.

[19] *New York Times,* December 9, 1970, p. 1.

[20] *New York Times,* October 17, 1969, p. 24.

[21] *New York Times,* March 7, 1970, p. 1; May 18, 1970, p. 20; May 19, 1970, p. 1.

[22] *New York Times,* May 9, 1970, p. 1; June 16, 1970, p. 16; June 17, 1970, p. 19.

[23] *New York Times,* May 20, 1970, p. 40. © 1970 by The New York Times Company. Reprinted by permission.

[24]*New York Times,* October 9, 1971, p. 35.

[25]272 U.S. 52 (1926).

[26]295 U.S. 602, 618–19 (1935).

[27]*Ibid.,* 628.

[28]*Wiener* v. *United States,* 357 U.S. 349 (1958).

[29]William L. Cary, *Politics and the Regulatory Agencies* (New York: McGraw-Hill Book Company, 1967), p. 7.

[30]Samuel P. Huntington, "Civilian Control and the Constitution," *American Political Science Review,* L, No. 3 (1956), 678–82.

[31]Richard Rovere and Arthur M. Schlesinger, Jr., *The MacArthur Controversy* (New York: Noonday Press, 1965), pp. 168–70.

[32]*Ibid.,* pp. 171–72.

[33]*New York Times,* January 18, 1961, p. 1.

[34]Robert J. Art, *The TFX Decision* (Boston: Little, Brown and Company, 1968), passim.

[35]Paul Y. Hammond, "A Functional Analysis of Defense Department Decision-Making in the McNamara Administration," *American Political Science Review,* LXII, No. 1 (1968), 57–69.

[36]John Kenneth Galbraith, *The New Industrial State* (New York: The New American Library Inc., 1968), pp. 181–89.

[37]*New York Times,* September 29, 1969, p. 1.

[38]*New York Times,* April 28, 1970, p. 18.

[39]Sidney Warren, *The President as World Leader* (New York: McGraw-Hill Book Company, 1967), p. 18.

[40]*Congressional Record,* 87th Cong., 1st sess., 1961, CVII, Part 1, 1012–13.

[41]*New York Times,* December 17, 1972, Sec. 1, p. 23.

[42]*Laird* v. *Tatum,* 408 U.S. 1 (1972).

f o u r

The President and the Supreme Court

Most of the time the president and the Supreme Court avoid decisions which could threaten a change in each other's authority and autonomy. On serious questions at least, they are content to leave one another alone. Their relationship is characterized by deference and, routine legal business aside, by distance. There is not much the president can do for the Court or the Court for the president; but each has the power to hurt or humiliate the other. Therefore the exchange most beneficial in the long run is not to interfere in each other's business. The president and the Court have come to value the constitutional gulf between them, in contrast with the tendency of the president and Congress to encroach upon each other's territory when opportunity arises.

The Supreme Court's powers command the respect of the White House. Early in the last century it assumed the power to find acts of the president and Congress unconstitutional. In the absence of a clear mandate one way or the other, the Court came to the bold conclusion that it must have final judgment on the faithfulness of the other branches of government to the words of the Constitution. The power of judicial review has made the Supreme Court of the United States a giant among the appellate courts of the world.

Certainly the Constitution does not say that the Supreme Court possesses a veto over the president or Congress. It is fair to assume that the state courts, and even the federal courts, were meant to strike down state laws and state executive decisions conflicting with the provisions of the federal Constitution and federal laws, but an intent to establish judicial review within the national government is arguable at best.[1] Alexander Hamilton supported the broader interpretation in the *Federalist* No. 78, but there is no direct evidence that the constitutional convention felt as he did.

Then, in the case of *Marbury* v. *Madison* in 1803, the Supreme Court asserted the power of judicial review over Congress for the first time.

> It is emphatically the province and duty of the judicial department to say what the law is. Those who apply the rule to particular cases, must of necessity expound and interpret that rule. If two laws conflict with each other, the courts must decide on the operation of each.
>
> So if a law be in opposition to the constitution; if both the law and the constitution apply to a particular case, so that the court must either decide the case conformably to the law, disregarding the constitution; or conformably to the constitution, disregarding the law; the court must determine which of these conflicting rules governs the case. This is of the very essence of judicial duty.[2]

John Marshall's argument flows to the conclusion that the Court must prefer the higher law of the Constitution to the acts of the president and Congress in case of conflict—yet only by assuming without proof that conflict can be diagnosed surely and objectively by the Court.

The power of judicial review remained unused for more than half a century, and was to be used vigorously only in this century, but it was not seriously questioned after *Marbury* v. *Madison,* except by an occasional student of legal history.

In addition to its formal authority as a court of last resort, the Supreme Court enjoys great prestige in the minds of the people, who tend to frame public questions in legal and constitutional terms and to look to the Court for answers. The British provide an instructive contrast in both regards: their courts lack the power to override the legislature or the executive on constitutional grounds, and the people themselves are less inclined to measure public issues against constitutional standards. The American habit of seeking constitutional solutions to political problems sustains the Court's extraordinary authority.

> So-called constitutional questions seem to exercise a mesmeric influence over the popular mind. This eagerness to settle—preferably forever—

a specific problem on the basis of the broadest possible constitutional pronouncements may not unfairly be called one of our minor national trends. An English observer of our scene has acutely described it: "At the first sound of a new argument over the United States Constitution and its interpretation the hearts of Americans leap with a fearful joy. The blood stirs powerfully in their veins and a new lustre brightens their eyes."[3]

Because of the Supreme Court's formal and informal powers, the potential for conflict with the president of the United States is unusually great. Stated in terms of the values controlled by each, the Court can leave the president's decisions and his legislative program alone or not, and the president, for his part, can interfere with the structure and operation of the Court or not. From the president's point of view the Court has its uses also. A Court dominated by the appointees of his predecessors is a good scapegoat; appointments to the bench are important as patronage for the reward of friends and for the appeasement of political factions; and an agreeable Court with a substantial number of his own appointees may be a more tractable legislative body than Congress and may reflect favorably upon the president.

The Norm of Judicial Deference

The motives for the Supreme Court's practice of allowing the president a generous measure of discretion, as expressed by the Court itself, fall into two groups: self-interest and self-denial. The interest of the Court in its own well-being is aroused by any danger that a decision will be ignored rather than obeyed by the president or that it will result in retaliation against the Court. Self-denial, on the other hand, is invoked by some members of the Court as a matter of principle, regardless of the hazards.

During most of its history there has been a working consensus on the Court, uniting justices of different persuasions, that the Court must avoid mortal combat with the president and Congress. Just enough conflict has occurred to keep the members of the Court apprehensive. As we shall see in reviewing deviant transactions when the two branches did not leave one another alone, Presidents Thomas Jefferson and Franklin Roosevelt both said they would ignore court decisions in some circumstances and were ready to attack the Supreme Court with impeachment or packing when its decisions embarrassed the White House.[4] Other presidents have worried the Court in other ways.

The ideological grounds for judicial deference to presidential and congressional authority have been set down in the written opinions of the advocates of judicial self-restraint—notably in the dicta of Justice Felix Frankfurter. While he shared the practical concern of his colleagues not to drift into political or technical entanglements and revive the antagonisms of the 1930s, Frankfurter's special contribution was to articulate the reasons why courts in a democracy should abstain from making policy. Briefly, he believed that the rules of law in constitutions and statutes require interpretation and reinterpretation in the process of application to concrete events—self-executing laws, he insisted, are an illusion. To interpret rules intelligently, one must weigh the interests at stake in each legal dispute as it arises. But in a democratic government, the legislature and the executive have far more expertise than the courts in weighing complex social values, and more legitimacy as spokesmen of the people. Frankfurter's standard approach to constitutional questions was to adumbrate the interests involved, typically with more insight than his more narrowly legalistic peers, and then to declare the unfitness of judges to deal with such complexities and to defer to the lawmakers and administrators who had made the decisions originally.

Frankfurter's contemporary and long-time intellectual adversary on the bench, Justice Hugo Black, took the position that most written rules were clear. Those contained in the Constitution were supreme and were to be applied fearlessly to all men—including the president, who enjoyed no immunity from the requirements of the fundamental law of the land. The two justices represented poles between which the majority of their Court wavered. Frankfurter argued for judicial restraint, even when the individual rights he valued highly as a private person were in jeopardy, and Black argued in a less complicated way for the strict enforcement of constitutional limitations on government.

As ideologists, both men at times incautiously ignored the nuances of exchange which helped their colleagues frame politically sophisticated decisions. Their performance on the Court, more in the service of principle than institutional self-interest, reminds us that an exchange model, or any other calculus of rewards and deprivations, has its limits as an explanation of human behavior. Departures from the exchange model seem more frequent in high courts than in other centers of decision in government, possibly because appointment for life permits Supreme Court justices to put matters of tenure and salary out of mind and to be uniquely unconcerned about pleasing superiors or voters.

Whether it is for purposes of self-interest or self-restraint, the Court's technical means of avoiding a struggle with the White House are abundant and effective. They give the Court control of its impact upon the presidency.

First, the Supreme Court refuses to entertain suits against the president himself—a limitation more symbolic than real because the president's agents who carry out his decisions have no such immunity. In an early case the justices held that it was proper for a court to order a subordinate of the president—in this instance the postmaster general —to heed the demands of Congress, even though the president himself was beyond the reach of the other branches of government, impeachment aside.[5] Some time later, when asked by the state of Mississippi to prevent Andrew Johnson from enforcing two allegedly unconstitutional reconstruction acts, the Supreme Court cited its earlier ruling and dismissed the case.[6] In fact a president's policies can be tested if the suit names an agent rather than the principal. When the steel industry sought to prevent President Truman from seizing its mills, it simply sued his secretary of commerce, the person designated to enforce the seizure order.[7]

The Supreme Court's other strategies for avoiding clashes with the president are less absolute in form but more effective in practice. Over the years the Court has perfected ways to refuse to hear cases and to give the president the benefit of the doubt in cases it does hear. When it declines to take a case, the Supreme Court need not give reasons, and rarely does. Most disputes brought to the Court are turned away with no more than the notation "certiorari denied" or a finding of "the want of a substantial federal question." Our insights into the Court's thinking are derived from an occasional majority or separate opinion.[8]

The Court has said, for example, that it will turn away "political" questions. In 1970 the Supreme Court declined to accept a case challenging the constitutionality of American involvement in the war in Indochina.[9] It gave no reasons. Had it done so, it is likely that it would have invoked the doctrine of political questions. What we know of the Court's decision comes from the dissenting opinion of Justice William Douglas, who felt the case should have been accepted for review in order to test the constitutionality of presidential war.

The plaintiff had argued that the United States could not lawfully participate in the war without a congressional declaration and called for appropriate restraints on the secretary of defense. In rebuttal the solicitor general, the president's agent before the Court, characterized the issue as one to be settled by the two political branches of government without judicial interference. Only Congress can determine whether it has declared war, he said, suggesting that the Gulf of Tonkin Resolution or other acts of Congress might have been deemed the equivalent of a declaration. Furthermore, he said, it would be disrespectful to go behind the president's statements to question his power to act in these circumstances.[10] The effect of the Court's refusal to involve itself in political questions is to keep it out of some of the most significant constitutional disputes of any generation.

Another issue that might well be avoided by the Court as "political," should it ever arise, is that of qualifications for the presidency. Herbert Hoover had not resided in the United States for fourteen years immediately prior to his election to the presidency. He could conceivably have been found to be unqualified under the provisions of Article II, Section 2 of the Constitution if the question had been taken up by the Court.[11] The same section of the Constitution specifies the puzzling requirement that the president be a "natural-born" citizen of the United States. Clearly native-born citizens are eligible and naturalized citizens are not, but the person born to United States citizens abroad may or may not be qualified.[12] He is a citizen, but not necessarily "native-born." A number of people who have been considered for the nomination in this century were born abroad: George Romney in a Mormon colony in Chihuahua, Mexico; Christian Herter in France; and Franklin D. Roosevelt, Jr., on an island in Canada, the summer home of his parents. Barry Goldwater was born in the territory of Arizona before its admission to the Union. Presented with the delicate question of the lawfulness of a presidential election, the Supreme Court might prudently defer to the decision of Congress, a "political" branch, in certifying the results of the balloting in the electoral college.

In a less drastic strategy of avoidance, the Court takes a case, assesses the merits, and gives the president the benefit of the doubt. One of the Court's favored rules of thumb is a strong presumption that the acts of president and Congress are constitutional. In less legalistic terms, the probability that the Court will decide against the president or Congress, once it has heard the arguments, is low.

When the President Acts Alone

The judicial review of Abraham Lincoln's war-time presidency offers a good illustration of the Supreme Court's customary restraint. Lincoln cautioned the Court in his inaugural address to expect the president to exercise leadership in the resolution of the grave constitutional issues of the day.

> ... The candid citizen must confess that if the policy of the government, upon vital questions affecting the whole people, is to be irrevocably fixed by decisions of the Supreme Court, the instant they are made, in ordinary

litigation between parties in personal actions, the people will have ceased to be their own rulers, having to that extent practically resigned their government into the hands of that eminent tribunal.[13]

He then assumed extraordinary authority as chief executive and commander in chief, including the power to suspend the writ of habeas corpus, to enlarge the army, to free slaves, to order military trial of civilians, and to blockade southern ports, thereby raising a tantalizing collection of questions for constitutional specialists. But some did not reach the Court, to its apparent relief; some were turned away; and the rest were decided heavily in the president's favor. The Court did not test the Emancipation Proclamation, for example. Its constitutionality was settled only by the ratification of the Thirteenth Amendment in 1865. And when it considered the claim of a civilian, Clement Vallandigham, that the army lacked authority to bring him to trial, the Supreme Court avoided a decision on the merits. Instead it took refuge in the procedural point that the decision of a military tribunal could not be reviewed by a writ of certiorari before the Supreme Court, and left the questions of military trials for civilians and the suspension of habeas corpus by presidential proclamation untouched.[14]

When it did reach an important issue in the *Prize Cases*—whether the president had acted properly in proclaiming a blockade of southern ports in the aftermath of the attack on Fort Sumter—the Court upheld the president squarely.[15] It rejected the argument that the consent of Congress in declaring war was a prerequisite to military action of this nature. Said the Court:

> The Constitution confers upon the president the whole executive power. He is bound to take care that the laws be faithfully executed. . . .
>
> If a war be made by invasion of a foreign nation, the president is not only authorized but bound to resist force by force. He does not initiate the war, but is bound to accept the challenge without waiting for any special legislative authority. And whether the hostile party be a foreign invader, or states organized in rebellion, it is none the less a war. . . .
>
> Whether the president is fulfilling his duties, as commander-in-chief, in suppressing the insurrection, has met with such armed hostile resistance, and a civil war of such alarming proportions as will compel him to accord to them the character of belligerents, is a question to be decided *by him*, and this Court must be governed by the decisions and acts of the political department of the government to which power was entrusted. . . . The proclamation of blockade is itself official and conclusive evidence to the Court that a state of war existed which demanded and authorized a recourse to such a measure. . . .[16]

But in 1866, once the war was ended and Lincoln dead, in fact one day after a proclamation from the White House that peace had been restored throughout the land, a divided Supreme Court found that the president had violated the Constitution in ordering military trials for spies and collaborators in the aftermath of his suspension of the writ of habeas corpus. The Court ruled in *Ex parte Milligan* that Congress might establish military tribunals to displace the civil courts in time of war; the president alone could not.[17] It was safe for the Supreme Court to be abrupt with the White House in 1866. A president who takes emergency action in the grey area of the Constitution probably should be content to know that the Court is unlikely to act against him during the emergency, or for that matter during his lifetime.

Since the Civil War the Supreme Court has held to this pattern, rarely interfering with presidential discretion, as a sampling of the fate of executive orders indicates.

In a case of Wild West romance and revenge in 1890, the Court upheld the right of the President and his agents to employ a deputy United States marshal as a bodyguard for a federal judge in California —in fact Supreme Court Justice Stephen J. Field riding circuit—despite the ambiguity of the Constitution and the laws on the matter. Justice Field had decided against the validity of the former marriage of a fiery woman who had already insulted and pulled the hair of one judge in the course of her litigation. She rose in Field's court at the verdict and swore that the judge had been bought, whereupon the judge ordered her removal from the room. Her husband then struck the marshal who was carrying her, knocking a tooth out, and was himself ejected by other marshals. Both received jail sentences for contempt of court. Once out of jail they made public threats on the life of Field, widely reported in the newspapers, inducing federal authorities to assign Marshal David Neagle to protect the judge. Not long after, spying the couple on a train with Field, the marshal alerted lawmen at the next stop and advised the judge to remain seated. But Justice Field boldly left the train for breakfast in a restaurant. There the husband stole up from behind, struck the judge twice, ignored the marshal's order to desist, reached for a weapon, and was shot twice and killed. The legal question was whether California could try the federal marshal for murder, or whether he might claim that he was acting under supreme federal law. Said the Court, "We cannot doubt the power of the president to take measures for the protection of a judge of one of the courts of the United States, who, while in the discharge of the duties of his office, is threatened with a personal attack which may probably result in his death. . . ."[18] The case is an important attestation of the president's discretionary authority.

The removal of more than 100,000 Japanese-Americans from the West Coast by military authorities at the beginning of World War II again tested the power of the executive to take action without explicit constitutional or statutory authority. By Executive Order 9066, President Roosevelt gave the military full discretion to remove dangerous persons from the coast.[19] Acting on this authority, later ratified by act of Congress, the army rounded up people of Japanese ancestry, citizens and noncitizens alike, and shipped them to camps in other parts of the country. Did the president have the authority to order the removal and incarceration of masses of people without a semblance of due process of law, on the sole basis of race? Again, and in the face of an array of constitutional complaints, the Supreme Court deferred to the political branches.

> We cannot say that the war-making branches of the government did not have ground for believing that in a critical hour such persons ... constituted a menace to the national defense and safety, which demanded that prompt and adequate measures by taken to guard against it. ...
> To find that the Constitution does not forbid the military measures now complained of does not carry with it approval of that which Congress and the executive did. That is their business, not ours.[20]

A year before, in the heat of war, the Court had avoided the question in a similar case. A Japanese-American had been sentenced to ninety days in jail for each of two offenses, violating a curfew and refusing to appear at a center for relocation. The sentences were to run concurrently. Upholding the curfew conviction, the Court said with an implicit sigh of relief that it need not go on to consider the more serious offense. The matter was moot—hypothetical—since the sentence had to be served in any event.[21]

Some months after authorizing the relocation of Japanese-Americans in the West, Franklin Roosevelt ordered an extraordinary military trial of German saboteurs caught in the East, and raised a new set of questions about presidential power in time of war. Two groups of Germans, all of whom had once lived in the United States, landed from submarines on the beaches of Long Island and Florida with explosives to be used against war industries and military facilities. Within two weeks every man had been picked up by the Federal Bureau of Investigation.[22] Without delay President Roosevelt issued a proclamation barring access to civil courts for persons who entered the country in time of war and were charged with acts of sabotage, followed by an executive order establishing a military tribunal to try such cases.[23] The prisoners were surrendered to the army, and it was generally assumed that a harsh example would be set.

Fearful that conviction and execution of the sentence might occur momentarily, counsel for the Germans rushed an appeal to the Supreme Court. The Court convened in special session to hear arguments, decided in favor of trial by the military, wrote a short opinion to be supplemented by a full opinion in due course, and returned to their summer vacations. Most of the saboteurs were put to death shortly after and two received prison terms. The full opinion issued months later.[24]

Members of the Court regarded their decision as an affirmation of the rule of law and the independence of the judiciary, for the Court had indeed ruled on the lawfulness of the procedures established by the president despite his determination to keep the civil courts out of the process entirely. But the urgency of the Court's consideration of the case was prompted by concern that the military intended to go ahead secretly and summarily with trial, conviction, and execution, and that if the Supreme Court wished to act at all it was well advised to offer a swift benediction. Faced with the alternatives of resisting a president who might ignore them in return and accepting his assumption of extraordinary authority at the expense of the civil judiciary, the Court chose the lesser humiliation.

A year after the end of the war, however, in a case resembling *Ex parte Milligan* in a number of respects, the Court reversed two wartime convictions handed down by military courts in the territory of Hawaii under the terms of a presidential order which had suspended the writ of habeas corpus and established martial law for the islands in the wake of the attack on Pearl Harbor.[25] One involved a civilian shipfitter convicted of assaulting two marine sentries at a navy yard, the other a civilian found guilty of the embezzlement of some stock. Justice Burton, in the minority, argued for caution in reviewing the decisions of the other branches of government: "For this Court to intrude its judgment into spheres of constitutional discretion that are reserved either to the Congress or to the chief executive, is to invite disregard of that judgment by the Congress or by the executive agencies under a claim of constitutional right to do so." But the majority of the Court were of the opinion that president Roosevelt's approval of martial law for Hawaii should have been construed by the military with care and with a decent respect for traditional constitutional rights. In the moment of emergency the governor of Hawaii had radioed the president for approval of his abrogation of habeas corpus and civil trials, and the president had responded by radio. "Not until 1943 was the text of the governor's December 7 proclamation furnished Washington officials," said the reproachful Court, "and it is still doubtful if it has been seen by the president."[26]

A logical reconciliation of the case of the saboteurs and the case of the civilians in Hawaii is not impossible—one involving enemy agents and a deliberate presidential action, the other resident civilians and a suspicion of presidential carelessness—but it is more realistic to regard them as inconsistent on the matter of access to civilian courts in war time. The case of the saboteurs was an instance of extreme judicial deference to the executive during an emergency, and the case of the Hawaiian convictions was a reassertion of the power of judicial review after the war was over and the president in question dead, in the pattern set by the Court at the time of the Civil War.

The *Steel Seizure Case* was a rare exception to the rule that the Court interferes with presidential discretion only when interest has died down. In the spring of 1952, President Harry Truman issued an executive order "directing the secretary of commerce to take possession of and operate the plants and facilities of certain steel companies" in order to prevent a strike that might hinder the prosecution of the war in Korea. The steel companies and the steel workers had conferred for many months about a new labor bargaining agreement without coming to terms. At the direction of the president, the Wage Stabilization Board had made recommendations, but these proved unhelpful. A nationwide strike was called, and the president seized the steel mills and reported to Congress on his actions. The steel companies went to court to attack the president's order. In the course of seven opinions spanning one hundred and thirty-two pages in the official reports, the Supreme Court presented the most thorough assessment of the power of the president it had ever written.[27]

In the opinion of the Court, delivered by Justice Black, there is a short, simple rejection of the view that the key phrases of Article II (that "The executive Power shall be vested in a President . . . ," that "he shall take Care that the Laws be faithfully executed," and that he "shall be Commander in Chief of the Army and Navy of the United States") give him discretion to seize the industry in the absence of congressional authorization.[28]

> The order cannot properly be sustained as an exercise of the president's military power as commander in chief of the armed forces. The government attempts to do so by citing a number of cases upholding broad powers in military commanders engaged in day-to-day fighting in a theater of war. Such cases need not concern us here. Even though "theater of war" be an expanding concept, we cannot with faithfulness to our constitutional system hold that the commander in chief of the armed forces has the ultimate power as such to take possession of private property in order to keep labor disputes from stopping production. This is a job for the nation's lawmakers, not for its military authorities.
>
> Nor can the seizure order be sustained because of the several constitutional provisions that grant executive power to the president. In the framework of our Constitution, the president's power to see that the laws are

faithfully executed refutes the idea that he is to be a lawmaker. The Constitution limits his functions in the lawmaking process to the recommending of laws he thinks wise and the vetoing of laws he thinks bad. And the Constitution is neither silent nor equivocal about who shall make laws which the president is to execute. The first section of the first article says that "All legislative Powers herein granted shall be vested in a Congress of the United States. . . ."[29]

Justice Black papered over some of the most interesting episodes in the history of the presidency in this schoolbook version of the theory of the separation of powers. But of the six members of the majority in this case, one refused to join in Black's statement of reasons and four chose to add qualifications and limitations in separate concurring opinions. Thus the "opinion of the court" was something less than that. In fact all of the justices but two—counting three dissenters and four members of the majority—adhered to the principle that under some circumstances the president does have emergency powers, although they differed on whether those circumstances were at hand. A majority took the narrow view of presidential authority in the opinion of the court, but a larger majority rejected that view. The result was a ruling that reversed one presidential decision without setting any firm precedent for the future.

However confusing the reasons they gave, the justices knew that Harry Truman had acted imprudently and could be resisted with impunity. The Taft-Hartley Act, passed in 1947, provided a mechanism for presidents to handle the threat of devastating strikes; but President Truman had opposed the act, vetoed it, watched a Republican Congress pass it over his veto, and campaigned for reelection in 1948 as an archcritic of Congress. Settling a strike by invoking Taft-Hartley was a humiliating prospect for the president. The partisan overtones of his choice of remedies, therefore, not to mention his low marks in the public opinion polls in 1952, the makeshift arguments of the Justice Department in defense of his action in court, and the feeling that a steel strike might not create such dangers in a stalemated war as the executive suggested, all worked against the White House. With some or all of these conditions absent, the Court would have had no trouble maintaining its habitual deference to the president.

When the President Uses Delegated Authority

The other great domain of presidential discretion recognized by the courts, in addition to his acting—or acting initially—on his own without statutory authority, is delegation. When it wishes, Congress gives the president and his appointees broad power to fill in the blanks in general legislation or to decide when and if legislative provisions will be invoked, and the judiciary has relaxed its strictures against excessive delegation accordingly. Congress may also legislate in detail to reduce the president's discretion.

Traditionally lawyers and political theorists have been concerned about the propriety of delegating legislative powers to the executive or to private persons because of the risk of upsetting the balance of a government of separated powers. In periods when this concern has coincided with an antigovernmental bias in the judiciary, the result has been close scrutiny of legislation for grants of power with too few strings attached.

The most striking judicial review of delegation occurred early in the New Deal, at a time when the Supreme Court was receptive to a variety of complaints against the validity of regulatory legislation. An important law passed in the first days of the Roosevelt administration, the National Industrial Recovery Act, established a system of government-business collaboration for industrial planning. In the "sick chicken" case, a unanimous Court voided the authority granted by the act to each industry in interstate commerce to draw up a code of fair competition, to have the force of law upon the approval of the president.[30] The petitioners were operators of a kosher poultry slaughterhouse in New York who had been convicted of eighteen violations of the Live Poultry Code. They had failed to adhere to the minimum wage and maximum hour provisions of the code, had taken unfair advantage of competitors by allowing customers to select chickens from a coop rather than selling an entire coop or a blind sample from it, and in one instance had sold an "unfit" chicken to a butcher. The key words in the NIRA, "fair competition," were too vague, said the Court, and the result was the delegation of authority to the executive—worse, to private industry too —that was properly exercised by the legislature itself. In a concurring opinion Justice Cardozo said that should this kind of delegation be permitted, "anything that Congress may do within the limits of the commerce clause for the betterment of business may be done by the president upon the recommendation of a trade association by calling it a code. This is delegation run riot."[31]

From this high point of the rule against excessive delegation the Supreme Court beat a steady retreat in the years that followed, first for foreign and then for domestic affairs. In 1936, a year in which it struck down major pieces of New Deal legislation, the Court was surprisingly permissive toward a congressional resolution empowering the president to decide if and when to stop the shipment of arms from the United States to certain warring nations in South America. The otherwise conservative Supreme Court sharply distinguished the power of the president in national and international affairs.

We are here dealing not alone with an authority vested in the president by an exertion of legislative power, but with such an authority plus the very delicate, plenary and exclusive power of the president as the sole organ of the federal government in the field of international relations— a power which does not require as a basis for its exercise an act of Congress, but which, of course, like every other governmental power, must be exercised in subordination to the applicable provisions of the Constitution. It is quite apparent that if, in the maintenance of our international relations, embarrassment—perhaps serious embarrassment—is to be avoided and success for our aims achieved, congressional legislation which is to be made effective through negotiation and inquiry within the international field must often accord to the president a degree of discretion and freedom from statutory restriction which would not be admissible were domestic affairs alone involved. Moreover, he, not Congress, has the better opportunity of knowing the conditions which prevail in foreign countries, and especially is this true in time of war. He has confidential sources of information. He has his agents in the form of diplomatic, consular, and other officials. Secrecy in respect of information gathered by them may be highly necessary, and the premature disclosure of it productive of harmful results.[32]

It continued:

When the president is to be authorized by legislation to act in respect of a matter intended to affect a situation in foreign territory, the legislator properly bears in mind the important consideration that the form of the president's action—or, indeed, whether he shall act at all—may well depend, among other things, upon the nature of the confidential information which he has or may thereafter receive, or upon the effect which his action may have upon our foreign relations. This consideration, in connection with what we have already said on the subject, discloses the unwisdom of requiring Congress in this field of governmental power to lay down narrowly definite standards by which the president is to be governed.[33]

But even in domestic matters the rule against delegation wore away in case after case. The statutory guideline for the president's appointees on the Federal Communications Commission in framing regulations for public broadcasting is the simple formula, "public interest, convenience, or necessity." When the National Broadcasting Company brought suit to enjoin the enforcement of chain broadcasting regulations promulgated in 1941, on grounds of overdelegation, the Supreme Court denied that the law conferred unlimited power upon commissioners. The standard "is as concrete as the complicated factors for judgment in such a field of delegated authority permit."[34] It may be noted that only two members of the Court at the time of the NIRA cases were still sitting when the more permissive NBC decision was handed down.

Shortly after that, the Court upheld the Emergency Price Control Act of 1942 against a similar challenge. Convicted of selling beef above the maximum price prescribed by the price administrator, petitioners contended among other things that the standards set by Congress for the guidance of the administrator were ill defined. The Court ruled that the legislation was adequate in this respect: "The Constitution as a continuously operative charter of government does not demand the impossible or the impracticable. It does not require that Congress find for itself every fact upon which it desires to base legislative action or that it make for itself detailed determinations which it has declared to be prerequisite to the application of the legislative policy to particular facts and circumstances impossible for Congress itself properly to investigate."[35] A flexible law allowing the executive branch to decide what prices shall be fixed and the levels at which they shall be fixed is as constitutional as a rigid law leaving them no discretion.

The moral is clear. The Court has abandoned the practice of denying the president and his subordinates gifts of discretionary authority from Congress. The comprehensive wage and price controls imposed by Richard Nixon in 1971 were based on provisions of the Economic Stabilization Act of 1970 delegating immense authority to the president. The key section in its entirety read:

§202.(a) The President is authorized to issue such orders and regulations as he may deem appropriate to stabilize prices, rents, wages, and salaries at levels not less than those prevailing on May 25, 1970. Such orders and regulations may provide for the making of such adjustments as may be necessary to prevent gross inequities.

(b) The authority conferred by this section shall not be exercised with respect to a particular industry or segment of the economy unless the President determines, after taking into account the seasonal nature of employment, the rate of employment or underemployment, and other mitigating factors, that prices or wages in that industry or segment of the economy have increased at a rate which is grossly disproportionate to the rate at which prices or wages increased in the economy generally.[36]

The act generously allowed the delegated authority to be freely redelegated to public officials of the president's choosing. "The President may delegate the performance of any function under this title to such officers, departments, and agencies of the United States as he may deem appropriate."[37] Congress could not foresee who would be doing what, or when it might be done, under the broad mandate of the act. There is some indication that the Democratic majority never expected the authority to be invoked by President Nixon, who had argued against passage of the legislation and, when it passed, promised not to use it.

There were other constitutional questions about the Economic Stabilization Act that might have been raised with effect earlier—a possible violation of the Constitution's prohibitions of legislative abrogation of private contracts, to mention the most obvious—that no longer interest the Supreme Court. Since most major domestic legislation is a product of presidential leadership, a rule to which the Economic Stabilization Act of 1970 was an exception, of course, the shift of judicial interest away from these questions is a boon to the president. Since 1937 the White House has enjoyed the luxury of having only to overcome the resistance of the legislature, without much worry about a judicial veto too.

The judicial revolution of 1937 represented a turning from the protection of property rights to the definition and protection of nonproperty rights. The Supreme Court effectively ceded authority to interpret the powers of government to the executive and legislative branches except in cases involving the Bill of Rights. In practice the Supreme Court saved the veto of judicial review for the transgressions of state and local governments. While the federal government's innovative regulatory legislation had incensed the old localistic, property-minded Court, it was invasions of the personal rights of the Fourteenth Amendment, and through it the First Amendment's freedoms of speech, press, assembly, and religion and the procedural rights of the remainder of the Bill of Rights, by sheriffs and state legislatures that drew the fire of the new Court.

Even now the president—directly or indirectly through his legislative program—runs afoul of the Constitution once in a while, it is true. Both Dwight Eisenhower and Richard Nixon were checked by the Supreme Court as they moved to enlarge their authority to combat domestic subversion. President Eisenhower extended the operation of an act of Congress, which gave certain agency heads extraordinary powers to suspend or dismiss employees, to the entire executive branch, sensitive and nonsensitive agencies alike. The Court found his executive order unwarranted. It reversed the suspension and dismissal of a food and drug inspector in the Department of Health, Education, and Welfare who had been charged with close association with persons "reliably reported to be Communists" and with giving time and money to alleged subversive organizations and attending their social gatherings. And it returned the act's coverage to the more sensitive agencies originally specified by Congress.[38] President Nixon was checked by a unanimous Supreme Court when he sought to justify warrantless electronic surveillance of domestic subversives. As we shall see below, the Court held that neither legislation nor the words of the Constitution granted him the authority to order wire-tapping and "bugging" without permission of a court.[39] And later, lower federal courts, in addition to deciding the Watergate and Ellsberg cases intrepidly despite White House pressures, rebuked the president for impounding funds, failing to seek confirmation of an agency director, and dismantling a statutory agency.

But cases of this kind are exceptional today. They are the sparks in an otherwise uneventful relationship of mutual deference. Neither side cares to return to the state of war of 1935–1937.

Abnormal Conflict of President and Court

The greatest sustained antagonism between the president and the Court occurred in the administrations of Thomas Jefferson and Franklin Roosevelt. In each case an activist Court posed a threat to the president, who retaliated with an attack meant to eliminate the threat and restore the norm of mutual deference.

After losing control of the White House and Congress to Jefferson and the Republicans in the election of 1800, the outgoing Federalists took steps to enlarge the judiciary (which had infuriated the opposition by vigorous enforcement of the Sedition Act against critics of the administration), to fill the new posts with Federalists, and to establish the courts as a stronghold of opposition to the new administration. President Adams requested and received legislation creating new inferior judgeships, relieving the members of the Supreme Court of the burden of circuit riding, and reducing the membership of the Court to five at the next vacancy in order to prevent the early appointment of a Republican. At their first opportunity, the Jeffersonians responded with pardons for people imprisoned under the Sedition Act and with new legislation which repealed the Federalist judiciary act in time to prevent the newly appointed judges from sitting, and which furthermore postponed the next session of the Supreme Court for fourteen months in order to discourage the new chief justice, John Marshall, from inducing his colleagues to find the repeal unconstitutional. By the time a test of the act became possible, predicted the Jeffersonians, the judges whose positions were at stake would have accepted their loss and the Supreme Court would find it difficult to rekindle the dispute.[40]

When at last the Court convened in 1803, it did indeed leave the Jeffersonians' legislation for the judiciary undisturbed, but went on to hand down a decision in the case of *Marbury* v. *Madison,* pending since 1801, that asserted the power of judicial review and proved to be of paramount importance in the relations of the Court and the other branches of government, as we have noted.[41] It was in all respects a political decision.

William Marbury was among forty-two people appointed justice of the peace in the District of Columbia by President Adams at the end of his term. Their commissions were signed and sealed, but the outgoing secretary of state, John Marshall, failed to deliver them in the rush of events during the Federalists' last days in office. The new secretary of state, James Madison, delivered some and withheld others on orders of the president. Marbury and three others asked the Supreme Court to force Madison to deliver their commissions. The practical problem confronting Marshall, now chief justice, was to avoid the embarrassment of either ordering the executive to take action and inviting refusal, or, alternatively, declining to reach a decision out of fear of such refusal. His solution was to decline the case, boldly and with full opinion, on the questionable technical ground that the act of Congress empowering the Supreme Court to issue orders—writs of mandamus—to the executive in response to suits brought to it directly, without prior recourse to lower courts, was an unwarranted enlargement of the Court's original jurisdiction set out in Article III of the Constitution. In dodging the dispute at hand in a display of self-denial, Marshall affirmed a far greater power for the Court.

Rather than leave it at that, however, the chief justice wrote a long sermon on the moral responsibilities of the president. Marbury had a right to his commission, he explained, and it was up to Jefferson rather than the Court to act.

> The government of the United States has been emphatically termed a government of laws, and not of men. It will certainly cease to deserve this high appellation, if the laws furnish no remedy for the violation of a vested legal right. . . .
> By the constitution of the United States, the president is invested with certain important political powers, in the exercise of which he is to use his own discretion, and is accountable only to his country in his political character, and to his own conscience.[42]

The net effect of the decision and the opinion of the chief justice was to enhance the Court's authority and embarrass the president and his secretary of state instead of the Court.

Although Jefferson and Marshall were cruelly critical of one another in private, their public contests at all times took the form of impersonal institutional conflict. Marshall lectured the executive in *Marbury* v. *Madison* in a lordly, general manner. Jefferson's response to the insults of the Court and the promise of more was quietly to encourage the destruction of the Federalists' judicial power by impeachment. The trial of an insane federal judge before the United States Senate was pushed forward with new vigor and completed with a verdict of guilty. Within the hour a justice of the Supreme Court, Samuel Chase, was impeached.[43] The trial soon began in the Senate. Jefferson and his agents in Congress planned to remove the members of the Court one by one, leaving only William Johnson of South Carolina, a loyal appointee of the new President, and to name Republicans to the vacancies.

Justice Chase had drawn just criticism for his intemperate anti-Republican remarks from the bench, but the offenses enumerated in his impeachment covered a broader range of "high crimes and misdemeanors," some related to real events, some fanciful. When the evidence had been adduced and the arguments presented for the prosecution and the defense, the Senators voted. To Jefferson's chagrin, Chase was acquitted on all counts because of defections among the Republicans. On some counts the margin was substantial; on one the vote was unanimous in favor of Chase. Marshall, who had appeared nervous and frightened as spectator and witness during the trial, knew that he and the judiciary were safe for the time.

Less than two years later, the chief executive and the chief justice clashed on a new issue. As a member of the Supreme Court and also in his role of circuit judge, Marshall presided at the trials of Aaron Burr and his associates for treason and related offenses. In a message to Congress before prosecution was begun by his subordinates, President Jefferson had declared his former vice-president guilty of attempting both to make war against Mexico and to induce the western states to break away from the Union. When Marshall decided the cases in favor of the accused, an enraged president asked Congress to impeach the chief justice, an ordeal from which Marshall was saved by the involvement of the government in urgent questions of foreign affairs.[44]

Twice during these proceedings Chief Justice Marshall subpoenaed the president, directing him to appear in court with certain documents Burr needed for his defense—alleged orders to the army and navy "to destroy" his "person and property." Jefferson resisted, convinced that the dignity of the presidency and a proper concern for the time-consuming responsibilities of that office required him to stay free of court orders, to which there would be no end if he once consented. Marshall was persuaded that the defendant's constitutional right to compel the attendance of witnesses was more important, and hinted that the president seemed to have time for vacations, which implied that he might also find time to give evidence in a capital case. Nothing came of the subpoena or its renewal later on, and the conclusion of the Burr trials put the issue to rest.[45]

With the help of the Republican press, John Marshall's popularity was to plummet in the aftermath of Burr's acquittal, then to rise case by case during his long tenure in office. The struggle with the executive branch was a time of testing and risk-taking which laid the groundwork of the judiciary as an equal among the branches of government. By surviving in a hostile environment, Marshall and the Court grew strong.

Both Jefferson and Marshall had to settle for less than they had wanted. Jefferson did not secure the impeachment and conviction of Marshall and the Federalist-dominated Court or the conviction of Burr. Marshall shied away from an unenforceable order to the executive in *Marbury* v. *Madison* and, not surprisingly, was disobeyed by Jefferson when he attempted a subpoena in the Burr case. Jefferson succeeded in frightening Marshall and the Court on a number of occasions, and with the repeal of 1802 proved that he could influence the conduct of its business by ordinary legislation. Marshall, on balance the victor, succeeded in maintaining a vigorous court despite some narrow escapes, and did a good deal more than anyone before or since to affirm the power and independence of the Supreme Court.

The lesson this judiciary and executive bequeathed one another was that each could be a formidable adversary, proud and vindictive. The demonstrated costs of conflict were enough to induce most presidents and Court majorities to adopt a respectful live-and-let-live attitude toward each other in the generations that followed.

The greatest conflict between the president and the Court thereafter occurred more than a century later in the New Deal, when a majority of the justices, unmindful of the bitter experience of the past, made unlimited war on the president's legislative program. The president's retaliation was neither swift nor sure, but effective enough to revive the norm of mutual deference.

Franklin Roosevelt's legislative program in the Hundred Days in the spring of 1933 and after was not tested in the Supreme Court until 1935. In the first months of that year the administration won some cases and lost some, but in May the Court struck down the Railroad Retirement Act, the National Industrial Act, and the Frazier-Lemke Act (for the relief of farm mortgagors) and went on to deny the authority of the president to remove members of independent regulatory commissions except as provided by Congress.[46] Roosevelt retorted that the Court was indulging in "horse-and-buggy" interpretation of the Constitution.[47] The following January the Court found the Agricultural Adjustment Act unconstitutional, reversed direction in February by upholding the Tennessee Valley Authority, and returned to form by invalidating the Guffey Coal Act in May.[48] The fate of the remainder of the legislation of the New Deal seemed dark.

Franklin Roosevelt won reelection in 1936 by a record margin. Confident that the people meant him to continue the work of the New Deal, he began a serious review of ways of curbing the judiciary that had been discussed intermittently for a number of years.[49]

In his campaign for the presidency in 1912, Theodore Roosevelt had advocated popular recall of judges and of *state* judicial decisions, giving the voters power to reject either at the polls.[50] The Progressives in 1924 would have given Congress authority, by an amendment to the Constitution, to reenact a statute to make it effective over a judicial veto. To these proposals the advisors of Franklin Roosevelt and members of the House and Senate added scores more, among them legislation limiting the Court's appellate jurisdiction or increasing its membership, and constitutional amendments requiring a qualified majority of the Court —or unanimity—in order to void legislation, allowing Congress to repass legislation found unconstitutional by the Supreme Court, and directly broadening the legislative authority of Congress. It was then that Attorney General Homer Cummings, who was writing a history of the Department of Justice in his spare time, discovered that conservative Justice McReynolds, as attorney general in 1913, had advocated a reform for federal courts other than the Supreme Court that might with fine irony be turned against the high court. McReynolds proposed the appointment of a new judge for every judge who reached the age of seventy, to maintain the efficiency of the judiciary. Six of the members of the Supreme Court, including McReynolds, were seventy or older. If it were enlarged by that number of liberals, the Court would give the president no more trouble.

Tactically, the campaign to pack the Supreme Court was a disaster. When Roosevelt slyly presented his plan to Congress as a program for helping the Court handle its ever-increasing work load, the chief justice told Congress that he and his brethren were not in need of assistance. "An increase in the number of justices would not promote the efficiency of the Court," he said.[51] The patent duplicity of the president lost him ground. Though full of dissatisfaction with the destructive tendencies of the Court, public and congressional opinion did not mobilize behind the president. The average American was ambivalent about the Court, damning its decisions and lauding it as an institution. Then "the switch in time that saved nine" occurred as Justices Hughes and Roberts voted with the more liberal members of the Court to sustain a state minimum wage law, a new federal farm mortgage act, a firearms tax, and provisions of the Railway Labor Act. Just how much they voted out of concern about criticism of the decisions of 1935 and 1936 one can only speculate.[52] A short while later the Court upheld the Wagner Labor Relations Act, to the relief of Congress and the White House.[53] When one of the conservative justices announced his retirement and Roosevelt's floor leader in the Senate died, the court-packing attempt, already in trouble in Congress, was lost.

The death and retirement of elderly justices soon gave the president an opportunity to remake the Court. The new Roosevelt Court handed down many bold decisions in its day, but it did not do battle with the president and his program. The norm was reestablished.

President Nixon and the Court

Because of the attention paid by the White House to the policies and composition of the judiciary in his administration, Richard Nixon's transactions with the Supreme Court are the most interesting of the post-New Deal period. Some of the relations can be classed as normal, but some appear as hurtful, deviant maneuvers.

The norm is embodied in the continuation of the truce of 1937. The Court, as we have seen, has refused to tamper with presidential authority in military and foreign affairs and in matters of economics and welfare at home. President Nixon has not given serious attention to any of the old plans for increasing the size of the Court or reducing its power, except with respect to school busing. But there has been friction in two areas of the law of some importance to President Nixon: wiretapping and the desegregation of the public schools. In both the Supreme Court unanimously disagreed with the president. His own appointees expressed their disagreement in writing as well as in voting.

In the one case, stemming from the dynamiting of a Central Intelligence Agency branch office in Ann Arbor, Michigan, the Court considered an assertion of the Justice Department that the president's agents might monitor telephone conversations in domestic security investigations without a warrant. The attorney general wanted unchecked authority to listen to the conversations of alleged subversives: government lawyers argued that wiretaps were a reasonable exercise of the president's power to protect the national security, and that neither the Constitution nor federal statutes required warrants in extraordinary cases involving an attempt to overthrow the government or any other clear and present danger to the structure or existence of the government. Without ruling on the constitutionality of wiretaps involving "foreign powers or their agents," the Court replied that neither the Constitution nor the Omnibus Crime Control and Safe Streets Act of 1968 cited by the government was intended to create an exemption from the established rules of search and seizure. "Given the difficulty of defining the domestic security interest, the danger of abuse in acting to protect that interest becomes apparent," said the Court. "We recognize, as we have before, the constitutional basis of the president's domestic security role," it concluded, "but we think it must be exercised in a manner compatible with the Fourth Amendment."[54] The decision left avenues of evasion—simple concealment of federal wiretapping, for example, or the transfer of wiretaps from the domestic category to the foreign by the allegation of links with foreign powers —but the President was sternly lectured on the rights of individuals and was told to mend his ways.

In the matter of public school desegregation the Supreme Court proved equally uncompromising. Late in 1969 President Nixon's secretary of health, education, and welfare asked a federal court for postponement of a desegregation order in Mississippi, the first time the government had been in court seeking a delay in desegregation. A few weeks later the Supreme Court unanimously denied the government's request in a curt *per curiam* opinion: ". . . continued operation of segregated schools under a standard allowing 'all deliberate speed' for desegregation is no longer constitutionally permissible."[55] The implicit message in the words of the Court was that in 1969 officials should not require a detailed explanation of reasons why it was time to live up to the original desegregation ruling of 1954.

Then in 1971 the Court repudiated the president's busing policy, again unanimously, this time in an opinion of the court written by Warren Burger, President Nixon's appointee as chief justice.[56] Earlier in a lengthy public statement the president had said that, while the constitutionality of busing as a means of school desegregation remained unsettled, there was no doubt in his mind of its undesirability —busing was onerous, wasteful, even racist in its implications, he said.[57] With this as its premise, the administration intervened as a friend of the court to discourage the adoption of a busing plan for Charlotte, North Carolina. But the Supreme Court approved busing as a lawful means of eliminating *de jure* segregation, a carefully circumscribed but unequivocal approval. The president's response was to use the discretion of the executive branch to narrow the impact of the Court's ruling. A desegregation plan formulated by the government for Austin, Texas, was disavowed as busing "for the sake of busing." A general warning was issued by the White House that federal officials who sought to impose massive busing were liable to be fired. And then the president asked Congress for legislation to prohibit new busing orders in the courts.[58]

In the wiretapping and busing cases the Court disregarded the strong preferences of the president and handed down rulings which could only be regarded as defeats for the executive. His responses were not unexpected: he took steps to neutralize the Court's rulings, reestablishing the *status quo ante.* The president's departures from the norm of restraint and deference toward the Court were designed to bring about a return to that norm by the Court.

The Nixon Nominees

In one respect, however, the relations of President Nixon and the Court deviated from the norm in purpose as well as technique. Some of his nominations to the Court suggested a desire to diminish the autonomy of the judiciary. Traditional values were in play too, including a reward to the South for its electoral support, but the uniqueness of President Nixon's nominations, particularly those rejected by the Senate or withdrawn by the White House in the heat of public criticism, was their lack of distinction. The deliberate avoidance of nominees with subtle minds suggested that the president wanted to build a tractable, predictable Court.

The lesson of the Eisenhower years was that half-way measures to change the outlook of the Court would not work. Early in his administration President Eisenhower set standards of appointment to the Supreme Court: "character and ability" foremost, clearance by the FBI and the American Bar Association, and, because he wanted judges "who commanded the respect, confidence, and pride of the population," no one with "extreme legal or philosophical views."[59] Within a few months of Eisenhower's inauguration the death of Chief Justice Vinson put the standards to the test. The president named Governor Earl Warren, who became one of the strongest judicial leaders in the nation's history, beginning in 1954 with the difficult feat of massing a divided Court behind a decision to desegregate the public schools. Chagrined that the Court should engage in social innovation rather than sticking to its judicial knitting—he was heard to characterize the appointment of Warren as "the biggest damnfool mistake" of his administration—President Eisenhower then added a further qualification of prior service on a lower federal court or a state supreme court for subsequent Supreme Court nominations, of which there were four.[60] Despite the narrowing of the field of candidates to judges of moderate philosophy who could survive the scrutiny of the FBI and the ABA, President Eisenhower's appointees on the whole gave the Court new brilliance and independence. He appointed a diverse lot and filled the fifth and last vacancy with a Democrat, true to his belief in "balance" on the Court.

To a severe critic of the Warren Court like Richard Nixon, the standards of appointment devised by Eisenhower must have seemed woefully inadequate. He replaced them one by one with new standards to prevent a renewal of the free-swinging liberalism of the Warren era. President Nixon's first appointment, Warren Burger to the chief justiceship, was routine and consistent with the Eisenhower guidelines— the promotion of a respectable conservative sitting judge. It was the next vacancy that marked the break with Eisenhower policy.

President Nixon named a bland senior federal appellate judge, Clement Haynsworth, to the seat abandoned by Abe Fortas in 1969, only to see the formation of a winning coalition opposed to confirmation in the Senate. The confirmation hearings documented the opposition of civil rights and labor organizations to the elevation of a man of Haynsworth's conservatism to the Supreme Court and revealed, as well, a degree of unconcern in the nominee about matters of ethics—deciding a case involving a firm in which he owned stock, for example—that many liberals and conservatives alike did not want to bring to the high court, especially in the wake of comparable disclosures involving sitting members of the Court.

The next nominee for the Fortas seat, G. Harrold Carswell, another conservative southern federal judge, was even less acceptable to liberals because of a judicial and an extrajudicial record of hostility to civil rights dating from the 1940s when he declared

> I am a Southerner by ancestry, birth, training, inclination, belief, and practice. I believe that segregation of the races is proper and the only practical way of life in our states, I have always so believed, and I shall always so act. I shall be the last to submit to any attempt on the part of anyone to break down and to weaken this firmly established policy of our people. . . .
>
> I yield to no man . . . in the firm, vigorous belief in the principles of white supremacy, and I shall always be so governed.[61]

In addition he was generally regarded in the profession as a jurist of less than average competence. Senators were not reassured by the explanation of Senator Roman Hruska: "There are a lot of mediocre judges and people and lawyers. They are entitled to a little representation, aren't they, and a little chance? We can't have all Brandeises and Cardozos and Frankfurters and stuff like that there."[62]

One theory of President Nixon's motivation in naming a man uniquely offensive to liberals and legal scholars was that he wanted, in the Senate's confirmation of Harrold Carswell, an unequivocal defeat of the forces that had opposed the confirmation of Clement Haynsworth and an unequivocal payment to the masses of his white supporters in the South. It seemed possible that the Senate, having spent itself on Haynsworth, would lack the will to renew its struggle with the White House. But Carswell was rejected, and the president sent a third name to the Senate, that of a respectable conservative judge from Minnesota who was confirmed without difficulty.

The president's wish to reward the South for its electoral support had been a normal political exchange. But in passing over the names of distinguished conservative jurists and in digging deep in the barrel for one of his nominations, President Nixon struck at the integrity and authority of the Court as well. Concurrently, members of Congress began to speak of the impeachment of Justice William Douglas in terms reminiscent of the campaign against Justice Samuel Chase in 1804. Senator Byrd of West Virginia had encouraged the House to begin proceedings if Carswell failed to win confirmation and, when that occurred, House Republican Leader Gerald Ford complied, almost certainly with White House consent or direction. It was clear that the President was determined to humiliate and weaken the Court. Justice Douglas was not impeached, as it turned out, but he was observed to abstain from many cases, apparently for fear of accusation of conflicts of interest, while his behavior was under investigation.[63]

Then the Court lost Justices John Harlan and Hugo Black in one week and with them much of its intellectual force. President Nixon was in a position to search for replacements of quality or to accelerate the drift of the Court toward commonness. He chose the latter. A number of men and women were considered by the White House and reviewed by the FBI and the bar association, including former Ku Klux Klan organizer, now senator, Robert Byrd and—the president's first choices —Judge Mildred Lillie of California and attorney Herschel Friday of Arkansas. Mrs. Lillie's reputation among members of the legal profession in California was undistinguished; Friday, a fellow bond lawyer and friend of Attorney General John Mitchell, was a member of a firm best remembered as a defender of segregation in the public schools of Little Rock. The bar association, whose standards were loose enough to allow approval of Haynsworth and Carswell, declared Lillie and Friday unfit for the Supreme Court. Only hours before the scheduled announcement of his final selection, the president decided to name Lewis Powell, a southern conservative of distinction, and William Rehnquist, an uncompromising Goldwater conservative in the Justice Department, to the vacancies to avoid the near certainty of two more humiliating defeats in the Senate. In the cases of Friday, Powell, and Rehnquist, the president abandoned Eisenhower's requirement of judicial experience, and in selecting Rehnquist he also dropped the rule against legal and philosophical extremism.

The motive of the president in recruiting people of the caliber of Mildred Lillie and Herschel Friday was clear enough. With two of his men on the Court, a shift to the right in decisions on criminal procedure had become apparent, but on the equally sensitive subjects of civil rights and the guarantees of the First Amendment the new Court had given no sign of repudiating the equalitarian and libertarian principles of the Warren era.[64] Furthermore, the progressively painful defeats of Haynsworth and Carswell had sharpened his determination to prove to the Senate and the public that he had not surrendered his leadership. He would force them to swallow bitter medicine, something he could not accomplish with nominees of recognized ability. He abandoned the possibility of mutually profitable rational exchange for the catharsis of retribution. With Lillie and Friday he would have humiliated the Senate, enhanced the relative authority of the presidency by demeaning the Court, and taken two steps toward the establishment of a dully predictable conservative Supreme Court.

Despite his assurances, one thing the president did *not* intend to do was to fill the Court with "strict constructionists." Strict construction in the sense of adherence to original constitutional meanings is impossible in most respects, for the key phrases of the Constitution were written broadly in order to bend with the times—there is no strict construction of "necessary and proper," "due process of law," or "equal protection of the laws." Strict construction in the sense of preferring old interpretations to new is possible, but hardly desirable to a modern president, who would find a return to old doctrines of nondelegation of legislative authority intolerable. And strict construction in the sense of judicial self-restraint, also possible, is something else the president did not want on the Supreme Court. He wanted, instead, a Court that would unashamedly promote the interests of the peace forces over the criminal forces, as he had put it, of the haves over the have-nots, and of the presidency over Congress. "Strict construction" had the ring of objectivity and respect for tradition; it was a genial deception. President Nixon's use of the term was reminiscent of Franklin Roosevelt's presentation of court-packing as a friendly effort to promote the efficiency of the judiciary.

Conclusion

Most presidents and Supreme Courts have found it wise not to attack each another for fear of mutual embarrassment or worse. Since the two have vast and imperfectly defined authority with which to threaten one another, and since neither needs the other's active support, the prudent exchange has been one of leaving each other alone.

Departures from this norm have tended to be short-lived. Transgressions of one branch provoke similar transgressions by the other, followed by a mutual retreat to established positions. President Jefferson's extended campaign against John Marshall's Supreme Court was of a different description, to be sure. Jefferson and his associates wanted to strip the Court of the power and the will to resist the political branches. Instead, Marshall asserted the Court's authority and independence and made the judiciary a coordinate branch of government. President Nixon attacked the Court through the power of appointment rather than impeachment, in an effort to reduce it to a subordinate status. Other presidents who have been at odds with the court have been content to aim for a reestablishment of normal equilibrium between the branches, but this phase of Richard Nixon's relation with the Court was more deadly in intent.

Franklin Roosevelt's provocation was greater than either Thomas Jefferson's or Richard Nixon's, but his remedy was milder. Court-packing was designed to make an unusually troublesome Supreme Court less troublesome, without reducing its legal authority and, as the quality of Roosevelt's appointments demonstrated, without bringing dishonor to the institution.

Notes

[1]Learned Hand, *The Bill of Rights* (Cambridge, Mass.: Harvard University Press, 1958), pp. 4–7.

[2]*Marbury* v. *Madison,* 1 Cr. 137, 177–78 (1803).

[3]Felix Frankfurter in *Youngstown Sheet & Tube Co.* v. *Sawyer,* 343 U.S. 579, 594 (1952).

[4]Robert Scigliano, *The Supreme Court and the Presidency* (New York: The Free Press, 1971), pp. 58–59.

[5]*Kendall* v. *United States* ex rel. *Stokes,* 12 Pet. 524, 609 (1838).

[6]*Mississippi* v. *Johnson,* 4 Wall. 475, 497–500 (1867). Presidents have allowed the use of their names in minor cases. See Glendon A. Schubert, Jr., *The Presidency in the Courts* (Minneapolis: University of Minnesota Press, 1957), p. 321.

[7] *Youngstown Sheet & Tube Co.* v. *Sawyer,* 343 U.S. 579 (1952).

[8] E.g., *Baker* v. *Carr,* 369 U.S. 186, 217 (1962).

[9] *Massachusetts* v. *Laird,* 400 U.S. 886 (1970).

[10] *Ibid.,* 886, 892–24.

[11] Charles Gordon, "Who Can Be President of the United States: The Unresolved Enigma," 28 *Md. L. Rev.* 1 (1968), 32 n. 241.

[12] *Ibid.,* p. 1.

[13] Carl Sandburg, *Abraham Lincoln: The War Years* (New York: Harcourt, Brace and Company, 1939), I, 132.

[14] Ex parte *Vallandigham,* 1 Wall. 243 (1864).

[15] 2 Bl. 635 (1863).

[16] *Ibid.,* 668, 670.

[17] 4 Wall. 2 (1866).

[18] In re *Neagle,* 135 U.S. 1, 44–53, 67 (1890).

[19] 7 Fed. Reg. 1407 (1942).

[20] *Korematsu* v. *United States,* 323 U.S. 214, 218, 225 (1944).

[21] *Hirabayashi* v. *United States,* 320 U.S. 81 (1943).

[22] Alpheus T. Mason, *Harlan Fiske Stone* (New York: The Viking Press, Inc., 1956), pp. 653–66.

[23] 7 Fed. Reg. 5101, 5103 (1942).

[24] Ex parte *Quirin,* 317 U.S. 1 (1942).

[25] *Duncan* v. *Kahanamoku,* 327 U.S. 304 (1946).

[26] *Ibid.,* 308 n. 2, 315, 343.

[27] *Youngstown Sheet & Tube Co.* v. *Sawyer,* 343 U.S. 579 (1952).

[28] *Ibid.,* 587.

[29] *Ibid.,* 587–88.

[30] *Schechter Poultry Corp.* v. *United States,* 295 U.S. 495 (1935).

[31] *Ibid.,* 553.

[32] *United States* v. *Curtiss-Wright Export Corp.,* 299 U.S. 304, 319–20 (1936).

[33] *Ibid.,* 321–22.

[34] *National Broadcasting Co.* v. *United States,* 319 U.S. 190, 214–16 (1943).

[35] *Yakus* v. *United States,* 321 U.S. 414, 423–24 (1944).

[36] 84 Stat. 799 (1970). In Executive Order 11615 the president leaves open the possibility that some authority for wage-price regulation may derive from other statutes or from the Constitution directly. 36 Fed. Reg. 15727 (1971).

[37] 84 Stat. 799 (1970).

[38] *Cole* v. *Young,* 351 U.S. 536, 540, 557 (1956).

[39] *United States* v. *U.S. District Court,* 407 U.S. 297 (1972).

[40] Albert J. Beveridge, *The Life of John Marshall* (Boston: Houghton Mifflin Company, 1919), II, 547–49; III, Chap. 2.

[41] 1 Cr. 137 (1803).

[42]*Ibid.,* 154, 163, 165–66.

[43]Beveridge, *The Life of John Marshall,* III, Chap 4.

[44]*Ibid.,* pp. 530–31.

[45]*Ibid.,* pp. 433, 444–45.

[46]*Railroad Retirement Board* v. *Alton Railroad Co.,* 295 U.S. 495 (1935); *Schechter Poultry Corp.* v. *United States,* 295 U.S. 495 (1935); *Louisville Bank* v. *Radford,* 295 U.S. 555 (1935); *Humphrey's Executor* v. *United States,* 295 U.S. 602 (1935.)

[47]William E. Leuchtenburg, "The Origins of Franklin D. Roosevelt's 'Court-Packing' Plan," 1966 *Supreme Court Rev.* 357.

[48]*United States* v. *Butler,* 297 U.S. 1 (1936); *Ashwander* v. *TVA,* 297 U.S. 288 (1936); *Carter* v. *Carter Coal Co.,* 298 U.S. 238 (1936).

[49]This account follows Leuchtenburg, "Origins of Court-Packing."

[50]Henry F. Pringle, *Theodore Roosevelt* (rev. ed.) (New York: Harcourt, Brace and World, 1956), pp. 390–91.

[51]Mason, *Harlan Fiske Stone,* p. 451.

[52]*West Coast Hotel* v. *Parrish,* 300 U.S. 391 (1937); *Wright* v. *Vinton Branch,* 300 U.S. 440 (1937); *Sonzinsky* v. *United States,* 300 U.S. 506 (1937); *Virginia Railway Co.* v. *System Federation No. 40,* 300 U.S. 515 (1937).

[53]*NLRB* v. *Jones & Laughlin Steel Corp.,* 301 U.S. 1 (1937).

[54]*United States* v. *U.S. District Court,* 407 U.S. 297, 320 (1972).

[55]*Alexander* v. *Holmes,* 396 U.S. 19 (1969).

[56]*Swann* v. *Charlotte-Mecklenburg,* 402 U.S. 1 (1971).

[57]*New York Times,* March 25, 1970, pp. 26–27.

[58]*New York Times,* August 4, 1971, p. 1; August 12, 1971, p. 1; *Congressional Quarterly,* March 25, 1972, pp. 639–40.

[59]Dwight D. Eisenhower, *Mandate for Change* (Garden City, N.Y.: Doubleday & Company, Inc., 1963), pp. 236–40.

[60]*Ibid.,* p. 230.

[61]Richard Harris, *Decision* (New York: Ballantine Books, Inc., 1972), pp. 25–26.

[62]*Ibid.,* p. 117.

[63]*New York Times,* December 9, 1970, p. 45.

[64]Philip Kurland, "1970 Term: Notes on the Emergence of the Burger Court," 1971 *Supreme Court Rev.* 265–322.

five

The President and Congress

To the vast disappointment of presidents, Congress has a tendency to respond coolly to requests for new domestic legislation from the White House. Negativism in Congress has a variety of manifestations, from the drama of a filibuster to the quiet failure of a Senate-House conference committee to reach a compromise, but underneath lies a firm sustaining judgment of the membership that the costs of enacting presidential proposals usually outweigh the rewards. Cantankerous personalities and procedural kinks that give an appearance of frustrating the will of the majority more often than not are symptoms of a consensus that the main business of Congress is the preservation of the status quo. Congress's obstructiveness is a calculated defense of favored interests at home in the states and congressional districts against the efforts of presidents to support new competing interests. Only in fiscal policy-making, when the health of the economy as a whole is thought to be at stake, rather than one part of the economy at the expense of another, is the president allowed some leeway.

An exchange model, which suggests that two branches of government will interact if both expect some gain, and not otherwise, is well suited to the president's transactions with an independent-minded institution skilled in trading favors. The usual competitive model, which tacitly or explicitly likens the interactions of the branches to a zero-sum game on the order of chess, the gains of one side balancing the losses of the other, fits less well. There are several reasons. Neither branch is likely to be enticed or coerced into defeat at the hands of the other. Politicians avoid zero-sum games when they can. Furthermore, members of Congress constantly engage in mutually profitable transactions among themselves and with others—conservative rather than redistributive, on the whole. It is implausible that a group adept at rational calculation of self-interest in some dealings should accept a less rewarding relationship with the president. Then, the simple Madisonian checks-and-balances view that each branch struggles to outdo the others and to prevent encroachments on its own constitutional domain does not account for the willingness of Congress to allow the president nearly perfect autonomy in foreign and military affairs. Exchange analysis on the other hand explains equally the obstructiveness of Congress in domestic matters and permissiveness in foreign affairs.

Congress is always willing to cooperate if the price is right. By comparison with, say, judges and military bureaucrats and others who may go against their own interests to satisfy the requirements of morality, ideology, or professionalism, members of Congress are devoted in an uncomplicated way to calculating gain before making decisions.

The president for his part normally plays the role of a trader in quest of profitable exchanges with Congress. Now and then presidents forego rational calculation for spells of impulsive or coercive behavior, as when Richard Nixon cudgeled the Senate in 1969 and 1970 to obtain personal gratification as much as to wear down opposition to his less attractive Supreme Court nominees. His efforts to trade favors had been crippled by faulty reports from his staff about which Senators could be persuaded and with what.[1] At other times presidents want to exchange but are uncertain how to do it. As we shall see, John Kennedy dissipated his resources in transacting with Congress and ended with bad bargains.[2] But these are exceptions. Normally the president is prepared—anxious—to engage in businesslike transactions with Congress.

A president's reputation depends above all on his ability to overcome the separation of powers and persuade Congress to enact his domestic legislative program. He may make a mark in other ways to be sure: style, popularity, and the way he deals with the misfortunes of war, civil strife, injustice, and scandal. It depends, too, on his record before taking office. A general as distinguished as George Washington or Dwight Eisenhower adds modestly to his reputation by honorable service as chief executive, and a people grateful for his wartime command forgive a General Grant his ineptitude in the White House. Thomas Jefferson, writing his own epitaph, described a man whose place in the nation's history, like Washington's, did not require election to the presidency: "Here lies buried Thomas Jefferson, author of the Declaration of American Independence, of the statute of Virginia for religious freedom, and father of the University of Virginia." Still, if a president is to achieve greatness in the White House, leadership of Congress is a test he cannot avoid.

Only the more passive Presidents—those who are agents of Congress, who follow rather than lead, who are content with the laws as they are —escape the frustrations that result from trying to move Congress. The usual pattern of interaction between a president and Congress is demand without response. Routine legislation and appropriations continue to be requested and supplied year in and year out, but serious White House leadership in domestic matters is, with rare exception, rejected by Congress.

But uncooperativeness is the rational alternative for Congress. Legislators tend to feel that bending to the will of the president, enacting his program, and assuring his reputation diverts attention from the more immediate concern of protecting the interests of important constituents and at the same time diminishes the autonomy and prestige of the legislative branch. Compared with the parliaments of the rest of the world, Congress is a powerful legislature. Yet its power is largely negative; its interests, structure, and procedures conspire to inhibit change and conserve existing law. Only briefly, in time of crisis, are the leaders of the legislature and the executive likely to recognize a supervening common interest in the passage of new laws. In normal times Congress refuses the exchange.

In the making of foreign and military policy, by contrast, Congress willingly allows the president broad discretion and the funding he requests. The norm is domestic policy-making by Congress, and foreign and military policy-making by the president. In a sense the agreement of the branches *not* to exchange, to leave internal affairs to one and external affairs to the other, is itself an exchange. But in the restricted sense of ongoing, voluntary transactions it is not. It is an avoidance of exchange, policed coercively, as we shall see, by periodic border wars between the branches that serve as reminders of the utility of separate spheres of influence.

Presidential Leadership

As legislative leader, the president has several instruments of persuasion at his command: messages to Congress, proposed bills, lobbying, the veto, and patronage. According to the Constitution, "He shall from time to time give the Congress Information of the State of the Union and recommend to their Consideration such Measures as he shall judge necessary and expedient. . . . " This is a power that has become a mandate for the president to set each session of Congress in motion with a State of the Union address describing his legislative program in general terms, and in the course of the session to deliver separate messages on major proposals—supported by draft legislation, technical information from executive agencies, and political engineering by the White House staff.

Thomas Jefferson was the first president to make a sustained effort to lead Congress. He honored the constitutional etiquette of his Federalist predecessors by avoiding visits to Capitol Hill except for ceremonial occasions, but he regularly invited legislators to the White House for dinner, and through his agents in Congress encouraged an exchange of intelligence between the branches so that he could know their needs and they his.

Jefferson's dinners for legislators were relaxed and informal. Food was brought to the president's side by dumbwaiter rather than by servants in order to preserve the confidentiality of the words that were spoken. And the president assuaged the inhibitions of status by dressing casually in well-worn trousers and a favorite pair of old slippers down at the heel, seating his guests at an egalitarian round table, and dishing out the food himself. It was a good setting for candor. He also brought the branches of government closer together by inducing friends to run for Congress and appointing recent members of Congress to executive posts.[3]

But his leadership of Congress failed when he tried to negotiate the passage of unpopular legislation. Jefferson had very little with which to bargain when the stakes were high: a trickle of patronage, perhaps, but less popular power and prestige than modern presidents, who can bid for some legislative support by putting campaign money, White House favor, and patronage behind the reelection of loyal congressmen.

Another innovator in legislative leadership was Woodrow Wilson, who built upon the precedent of Jackson, Lincoln, and other strong presidents and avoided some of the mistakes of the weak. His immediate predecessors, Theodore Roosevelt and William Howard Taft, epitomized the alternatives. Roosevelt wrote:

> I declined to adopt the view that what was imperatively necessary for the nation could not be done by the president unless he could find some specific authorization to do it. My belief was that it was not only his right but his duty to do anything that the needs of the nation demanded unless

such action was forbidden by the Constitution or by the laws. . . . I did not usurp power, but I did greatly broaden the use of executive power.[4]

Taft's view was different:

> The true view of the executive function is, as I conceive it, that the president can exercise no power which cannot be fairly and reasonably traced to some specific grant of power or justly implied and included within such express grant as proper and necessary to its exercise. Such specific grant must be either in the federal Constitution or in an act of Congress passed in pursuance thereof. There is no undefined residuum of power which he can exercise because it seems to him to be in the public interest. . . .[5]

Wilson's strategy was to collaborate with Congress rather than act alone, and to bring the weight of public indignation to bear on the legislature when it proved intractable. He increased the bargaining power of the White House appreciably.

President Wilson revived a tradition from the days of John Adams by delivering important messages to Congress in person. He followed the progress of bills or portions of them in which he had an interest, and he went to Capitol Hill to work for their passage, occupying the President's Room for the purpose, to the surprise of legislators and against the firm advice of friendly legislative leaders. He even had a special telephone installed to connect the White House and the Senate.[6]

Unlike Jefferson, who could offer direction to a Congress largely free of indigenous leadership, Wilson faced a legislative oligarchy as entrenched as any in the nation's history. He chose to work through the leaders of the two chambers and their standing committees, and to put the force of the Democratic party caucus in each house behind his legislation rather than to mobilize progressives across party lines.

Today, collaboration with congressional leaders and regular contact between the White House and ordinary members of Congress, experimental in Wilson's administration, is routine. Under John Kennedy and Lyndon Johnson, when the two branches were controlled by the same party, congressional affairs for the entire executive branch were coordinated by Lawrence O'Brien, a presidential assistant. O'Brien gathered weekly reports from each agency on its contacts with Congress during the week before and concerning its plans for the following week, prepared a summary for the president's use in a weekly meeting with legislative leaders, and periodically brought together the forty or so legislative liaison specialists in the executive for strategy sessions in support of the president's program.[7]

O'Brien had a reputation of competence in informing Congress and the White House of one another's interests and of trustworthiness as an intermediary. The dramatic variability in White House fortunes with legislation during his tenure suggest, however, that these skills are less important than the fluctuations of bargaining power in the two branches from session to session. White House monitoring of the legislative process is now so much a matter of course that a president is open to public criticism if his agents falter. One day during the Nixon administration, for example, while the chief White House aide for congressional relations was watching a football game in New England and his assistants were dispersed in other directions, the Senate for the first time defeated the annual foreign aid bill, quite unexpectedly. Liberal and conservative critics of different aspects of foreign aid had come together in a vote that was embarrassing to the administration internationally and among political professionals at home. The vote was reversed not long after, with White House pressure back to normal once again.

There was a memorable test of White House influence on Capitol Hill in Richard Nixon's first term. When it became clear that President Nixon's nomination of Judge Clement Haynsworth to the Supreme Court was in trouble in the Senate, jeopardizing the president's reputation and leadership, the White House set in motion the full machinery of presidential persuasion.[8] Direct and indirect pressures were put on members of the Senate to convince them that cooperation with the president would be the more profitable choice. Massive efforts by the White House in the constituencies helped to turn senatorial mail, which had been running heavily against confirmation, in favor of Judge Haynsworth. Important constituents were induced to telephone their senators. And where carrots failed, presidential aides used sticks, threatening to run strong opponents in forthcoming primaries, to withdraw the president's personal and monetary support in the general election, and to stall public works expenditures selectively. Fence sitters were invited to the White House to talk with the president, and some were led to believe that access to the White House might be cut off if they voted the wrong way. As one senator said, "I expect pressure. I know we're not playing beanbag down here. But some of this was rough." Administration persuasion and coercion was so pervasive, in fact, that a number of Senators reacted publicly. A freshman Republican, for example, reported the veiled threat that a detailed review would be made of the income tax returns of senators who voted against the president. He characterized the pressure campaign of the White House in favor of confirmation and organized labor's opposition as equally "ham-handed." When at last the vote went against the administration, the blow was all the greater for the fury of the president's efforts. A while later the story was faithfully reenacted, chapter by chapter, in the struggle over the confirmation of G. Harrold Carswell, with promises of public works, campaign support, judgeships for senators' friends, and so forth, ending in a defeat that drove the prestige of the administration to a new low.[9]

One lesson of the rejected confirmations was that the president should have chosen candidates with fewer blemishes. Another was that he should not have relied too heavily on appeals to party regularity and personal loyalty, because he had relatively little to offer members of the Senate. Presidents always have difficulty translating debts to legislators into the currency of political exchange. Tangible patronage at the president's disposal is greater now than in the early days of the republic, certainly, but it is still limited. Legislators are aware that their political careers are only incidentally dependent upon the goodwill of the president. Still, to mobilize its limited resources, the White House some time later announced its intention to select departmental lobbyists itself in the future, rather than leave their appointment in the hands of departmental officials.[10]

The Constitution gives the president a veto upon acts of Congress, a negative where positive leadership has failed. But the veto is not final, since it can be overridden by Congress and has been on important occasions. And it is applicable only to entire acts. The president, unlike a governor with his item veto, cannot strike an offending provision from an otherwise acceptable measure. (He may refuse to spend funds after they have been appropriated, however. Harry Truman angered Congress by impounding military appropriations he thought excessive. Richard Nixon impounded many billions in domestic appropriations for housing, mass transit, and other programs.[11] He went so far in his second term that members of Congress joined in a successful suit in federal court to release certain funds and took steps to clarify the obligation of the president to spend appropriations in the future.)[12]

The veto, or the threat of a veto, is a favorite device of presidents who wish to dominate Congress. Franklin Roosevelt averaged a veto a week during his twelve years in office.[13] He would ask his advisors for a measure to veto as a display of strength, even if the bill had to be taken from the approved list of agency bills consistent with his program. Roosevelt, like Richard Nixon, seemed to believe that a certain randomness in presidential decisions, like strokes of lightning, increased respect for the office.

The veto may discourage Congress from sending some undesirable pieces of legislation to the White House, but it is not an instrument of affirmative leadership. In a sense Congress is itself by inclination a vetoing body. If at one time the central function of Congress was conceived to be policy-making, subject to presidential veto, it is now the president who is the prime innovator, subject to the veto of Congress. When the main legislative activity of Congress is saying no to the president, the president's veto is of marginal significance. President Nixon's campaign to hold down domestic spending by vetoing and impounding the appropriations of a Democratic Congress was a notable departure from this norm.

A spectacular veto occurred in 1944. President Roosevelt and the Treasury Department had pressed for tax reform, only to have the Ways and Means Committee of the House of Representatives reject its proposals out of hand and ungraciously bar treasury officials from its closed-door deliberations. To Roosevelt the House substitute bill was a triumph of special interests over the general interest, inadequate as a revenue measure, and dangerously inflationary. The Senate concurred with the House and sent the measure to the president for signature. Roosevelt vetoed the bill and wrote an acid explanation. It was "not a tax bill but a tax relief bill providing relief not for the needy but for the greedy," he said. "It has been suggested by some that I should give my approval to this bill on the ground that having asked the Congress for a loaf of bread to take care of this war for the sake of this and succeeding generations, I should be content with a small piece of crust. I might have done so if I had not noted that the small crust contained so many extraneous and inedible materials. . . ."[14]

In the Senate, Majority Leader Alben Barkley, already sensitive to charges that he and his colleagues had become presidential lackeys, angrily announced his intention to resign. The veto message, he said, was a "calculated and deliberate assault upon the legislative integrity of every member of Congress. . . . If the Congress of the United States has any self-respect left," he continued, "it will override the veto of the president. . . ." The president responded with a saccharine note asking Barkley not to resign but hoping for his unanimous reelection if he should. Resignation and unanimous reelection ensued according to the script, the veto was overridden, and the president and his legislative leader, now a hero in the Senate, made peace and resumed their cordial relationship.

Another constitutional power of the president, also of limited effect, is his authority to convene Congress. Franklin Roosevelt used it when he took office to bring Congress into emergency session to deal with the depression. Harry Truman used it not to legislate but to prove to the electorate that Congress was unprepared to legislate. After a year and a half of sparring with a Republican Congress unwilling to pass his program but bold enough to pass a major piece of labor legislation, the

Taft-Hartley Act—over his veto—President Truman called it into session during his 1948 campaign, asked it to act on housing, civil rights, health care, a higher minimum wage, public power, and displaced persons, and when—predictably—it did not, he flayed it as the "Republican do-nothing Congress" with great effect. It was good sport and it won votes.

Congressional Response— Legislation

A president who makes serious demands of Congress is almost certain to be disappointed. He should hope for a brief moment of cooperativeness at most. The presidency of John Kennedy illustrates some of the problems.

Kennedy regarded leadership of Congress as a prime test of presidential ability. His campaign statements, in the tradition of strong presidents, stressed the need for national action in the service of liberal values.

> The times—and the people—demand ... a vigorous proponent of the national interest—not a passive broker for conflicting private interests. ... They demand that he be the head of a responsible party, not rise so far above politics as to be invisible—a man who will formulate and fight for legislative policies, not be a casual bystander to the legislative process.[15]

The election, however, gave him the narrowest of popular margins and a Congress containing some two dozen more Republicans than the last. On strict party lines the president had a modest working majority, but in reality he could expect conservative opposition to his program within his party, more than offsetting the support of liberal Republicans. On balance his leadership of Congress seemed to be in jeopardy.

He did four things. First, he decided against immediate action on a good deal of his domestic program. Perhaps as a realist he wanted to avoid premature consideration of controversial measures like civil rights and medical care for the aged, keeping the issues alive in the hope of passage later in his administration or, with a new popular mandate for himself and Congress, in 1965. Perhaps he abandoned his New Frontier.[16]

Second, he chose to appease the South, in an effort to win the support of southern Democrats in Congress, by appointing conservative southerners to the federal bench, postponing executive action in defense of civil rights, watering down a minimum wage proposal for the benefit of southern employers, increasing support for cotton, and securing accelerated public works legislation and special rural aid measures for depressed areas.

Third, as we shall see in some detail later, he tried to relax the grip of the conservative House Rules Committee on liberal legislation. And fourth, he stepped up the lobbying efforts of the White House from the quiet routine of the Eisenhower years to an unabashed campaign of rewarding loyalty in Congress. White House aide O'Brien tabulated the votes of each legislator, assigning people to observe nonrecord voting when necessary; let favored members of Congress announce the award of federal contracts in their districts; sent letters of appreciation, birthday notes, presidential photographs, and invitations to the White House; and dispensed campaign support, public works, and patronage selectively.

Nevertheless the Kennedy presidency amounted to three years of tentative leadership from the White House and cold rejection by Congress. Only a few significant measures were passed, predominantly in foreign affairs, such as the establishment of the Peace Corps, the Alliance for Progress, and the Arms Control and Disarmament Agency; area redevelopment; manpower development and training; and the Trade Expansion Act. Compared with his successor, John Kennedy fared badly as the country's chief legislator.

Either the odds against him were too heavy or he failed to adopt the best strategy. He faced a difficult Congress, unquestionably, with an inauspicious party alignment; a seniority system burdening him with old, typically southern, committee chairmen; antagonisms between the House and the Senate; a majority of his party on the Hill used to opposition because they had not served under a president of their party; many legislators resentful of the sudden shift of public attention to the White House; and, with the death of Speaker Rayburn in 1961, uninspired leadership in both chambers under John McCormack and Mike Mansfield. But there remains the suspicion even among his friends that the president's response was not one of salvaging all he could in a bad situation so much as appeasement, retreat, and the alienation of his friends in Congress. If so he was a poor bargainer.

In the Kennedy administration the ratio of legislative victories and defeats was an unhappy exaggeration of the normal pattern of executive-legislative exchange: a middling level of cooperation, declining after a honeymoon period in each administration. Of all the presidents in the last generation, Lyndon Johnson was the most successful leader of Congress in two respects: he enjoyed a productive relationship at the outset and he maintained it. John Kennedy's leadership of Congress was fairly weak to begin with and it reached a low in his last year.[17]

Even a modest response of Congress to the president's requests can be deceptive if the legislation and accompanying appropriations are either parsimonious or unusually detailed. Not infrequently Congress passes an act full of promise and hobbles it with inadequate funding and enforcement. Civil rights legislation is chronically subverted in this manner. The direction of President Kennedy's Alliance for Progress, a grand revamping of aid to Latin America, was more in the hands of conservative congressional committees than the executive. Kennedy's aide Arthur Schlesinger ruefully cites Madison's description of Congress in the *Federalist* No. 48: "Its constitutional powers being at once more extensive, and less susceptible of precise limits, it can, with the greater facility, mask, under complicated and indirect measures, the encroachments which it makes on the coordinate departments."[18]

In the early New Deal, Congress delegated authority to the president in broad terms and left him a good deal of discretion in spending large lump-sum appropriations. It still does in some cases, without interference from judiciary now. In other cases Congress legislates in detail, at the expense of presidential discretion, often by granting authority directly to his subordinates. When it does delegate unstintingly to the president, the reason may not be to enhance his effectiveness. When Congress exempted private clubs from antidiscrimination provisions of the 1964 Civil Rights Act it declined to offer guidelines. Knowing the technical and political difficulty of resolving the distinction between public accommodations and private facilities, Congress delegated the problem to the president, his subordinates, and the courts. The vast delegation of authority underlying President Nixon's wage-price freeze in 1971 was also intended to be an embarrassment rather than a benefit. A Democratic Congress passed the measure with every hope of being able to accuse the Republican president of failure to make use of existing anti-inflationary legislation. But President Nixon, after long denying that he would impose controls, stole Congress's thunder by invoking the authority.

The normal effect of legislative parsimony and specificity is to limit the president to making marginal changes, at most, in federal policy. In general Congress's refusal to cooperate freely with the White House leads to conservatism in domestic affairs, and may in compensation induce presidents to devote more energy to experimentation in international affairs. Since the New Deal, innovations in federal policy have tended to occur without the involvement of Congress, by the courts or by the president acting alone.

Congressional Response—
War Powers and Confirmation

Congress can engage in bargaining and exchange with the president in several areas apart from legislation and appropriation, including the supervision of executive agencies and investigation of their problems, the declaration of war, ratification of treaties, and confirmation of appointments to executive and judicial posts. As a rule the response of Congress has been one of noninterference in these matters in recognition of a set of concerns that are in effect the property of the executive. There is a parallel in the development of the doctrine of political questions by the Supreme Court to establish separate spheres of influence for the judicial and "political" branches of the government.

In foreign and military affairs the power of the president is now supreme, despite provisions of the Constitution requiring the consent of Congress, despite the tragic experience of a presidential war in Indochina and the moral and legal criticism it has provoked. The Constitution grants the president broad powers over war and peace, but it balances them with the power of Congress to declare war and to ratify treaties, as well as with general controls through legislation, appropriation, and confirmation. During the Vietnam War there was an occasional threat to use the powers of legislation and appropriation to limit presidential discretion, but no evidence that a majority in Congress would vote for serious or immediate curbs.

As the war in Indochina enlarged during the 1960s, it was liberal members of the Committee on Foreign Relations, under the direction of Senator J. William Fulbright, who became the most vocal critics, captured headlines and television time, and helped to mobilize public opinion against the war. But Fulbright's impact was on the public rather than on the Senate.

Only once in the course of the war was a firm constraint placed upon the war powers of the president by both houses of Congress together. When President Nixon directed the invasion of Cambodia in 1970 without so much as notifying the Foreign Relations Committee, the Senate passed the Cooper-Church Amendment to cut off funds for American ground and air action in the area immediately. After a long debate a weaker version allowing continued air support for Cambodian forces passed the House and Senate. But when Senators McGovern and Hatfield proposed a measure to apply the same sanction of cutting off funds to the larger war at the end of 1971, prohibiting their use for maintaining American troops or continuing American military operations in Indochina, it was defeated 42 to 55.[19]

The next resort of the war critics was the Mansfield Amendment, first adopted in 1971 as a rider in a bill to extend the draft, declaring it to be the policy of the United States to end military operations in Indochina as soon as possible, and providing for withdrawal in nine months, subject to the release of American prisoners of war. When the House of Representatives balked at the nine-month limit, a conference committee eliminated the provision, and the compromise measure passed both houses. A second Mansfield Amendment was attached to a defense procurement bill later in the year, calling for withdrawal within six months. Again the deadline was removed in conference committee, and a weak version declaring only that it was the policy of the United States to withdraw from Indochina by a date to be set by the president was sent to the White House. In signing the act, President Nixon stated his intention to ignore the amendment. "To avoid possible misconceptions," he said, he wished to emphasize that it "does not represent the policies of this administration. . . . It is without binding force or effect, and it does not reflect my judgment about the way in which the war should be brought to a conclusion."[20]

Rebuffed by the president, Senate liberals turned their support to a proposal of Senator Jacob Javits to require the president to solicit specific congressional approval of a commitment of American troops— to protect American civilians or military forces, for example—within thirty days. But in order to obtain the votes for passage, Senator Javits accepted an amendment exempting the war in Indochina from its requirements![21] Further, all of the senators knew that the proposal would not clear the House while the war was on. Some, including Senator Fulbright, felt that it gained nothing and conceded the president unwarranted emergency authority to commit the nation to war single-handedly. In 1973, as massive American bombing continued in Indochina despite a cease-fire in Vietnam, Congress at last negotiated a compromise settlement with a president reeling from Watergate disclosures, to end American military involvement later in the year.

Certainly the formal power to declare war is not what it once was. The last declaration of war by Congress was on December 8, 1941, a day after the Japanese attack on Pearl Harbor. Since then American forces have become involved in bloody wars in Korea and Indochina at the initiative of the president, and presidents under fire at home have elaborated their defenses of undeclared war. Perhaps the least persuasive of these were the manly assertions of presidential prerogative.

I would say that the American people have elected as their president a man who is determined to honor our commitments, a man who is determined to stand with the people of Vietnam, stand with them until aggression has been ended and until the American soldiers can proudly come marching home. . . .

Now there are many, many, who can recommend and advise and sometimes a few of them consent. But there is only one that has been chosen by the American people to decide. . . .

[D]on't let [the leaders of North Vietnam] think because some senator says on a television program he is going to put the heat on the president that we will not persevere.[22]

The more legalistic arguments for American involvement fell into five groups: the protection of American civilian and military personnel, treaty obligations, the invitation of an ally under attack, congressional consent other than a declaration of war, and the abundant historical precedent of military action without a declaration.[23] Skeptics in the Senate, for their part, questioned each of these contentions: the "protection" of Americans in a war zone who might have been withdrawn entirely as an alternative, the force of a treaty "obligation" which other signatories did not recognize, the legitimacy of an invitation from a puppet government, the lawfulness of substituting other congressional procedures for a declaration of war, and the authority of erroneous precedent. After listening to a State Department witness on the subject in 1967, Senator Eugene McCarthy remarked, "This is the wildest testimony I ever heard. There is no limit to what he says the president could do. There is only one thing to do—take it to the country."[24] Which he did.

Beneath the legalisms it became evident as the war in Vietnam went on that the government believed it had a roving commission to fight communism where it found it. As Secretary of State Rusk put it in 1966, "No would-be aggressor should suppose that the absence of a defense treaty, congressional declaration, or U.S. military presence, grants immunity to aggression."[25] The declaration of war was obsolete.

Whether or not military appropriations and other ordinary legislation in support of a controversial war are the equivalent of a declaration of war, the fact is that congressmen prefer not to try to pull themselves together for a showdown with the president. And they know there is support among the voters for the continuance of unfettered executive discretion in international affairs.[26]

The treaty powers of the Senate are equally eroded. When the president anticipates substantial opposition to an international agreement in the Senate, he now concludes it without advice and consent in the form of an executive agreement. Within the last generation executive agreements have become the norm and ratification by Congress the exception. When President Nixon prepared to renew an executive agreement with Spain in 1969, accepting leases to military bases in that country in exchange for military equipment valued at fifty million dollars and other considerations, members of the Senate Foreign Relations Committee raised a number of objections: the trade seemed disadvantageous to the United States, it implied a commitment to support the Franco dictatorship, and the agreement—if any—ought to take the form of a treaty. The administration gave assurances that American commitments were not being enlarged and proceeded to renew the executive agreement. There was no serious objection in the Senate.[27]

In the early 1950s the Senate considered and narrowly rejected several versions of an amendment to the Constitution proposed by Senator John Bricker, and substitutes offered by other conservatives, to place curbs on international agreements and their enforcement within the United States.[28] Most versions of the amendment would have brought executive agreements under the control of Congress by broad enabling acts or other unspecified means. (Some legal scholars were as critical of the ambiguity of the language as of the substance of the limitations.) But after a series of votes in 1954, the Senate abandoned the effort to pass the amendment.

Congress normally is passive about executive appointments also, although as in the case of war and foreign affairs it has the authority to demand that power be shared. The Constitution provides for Senate confirmation of presidential appointments to important executive and judicial positions, the exact coverage of the provision to be controlled by Congress. By custom, the weight given by the president and the Senate to each other's preferences varies according to the office. Most presidents are allowed to select a cabinet without interference; confirmations tend to be perfunctory even when the nominees favor public policies repugnant to a majority of the legislators. Supreme Court appointments have become less perfunctory of late and more like those to independent regulatory commissions than to the cabinet. The Senate shows more interest in questions of ethics and even ideology, on the theory that the membership of these institutions, unlike the cabinet, is the close concern of the legislative branch too. Finally, appointments to a third group, outlying executive positions and federal district and appellate judgeships, are under the patronage of the senators of the state where the appointee will work—usually the senior senator of the president's party, according to the tradition of senatorial courtesy.

Earnest opposition to a cabinet nomination is so rare that when it occurs, people are apt to remember it long after. President Eisenhower's nominee for secretary of commerce, Atomic Energy Commission Chairman Lewis Strauss, was turned down by a vote of 46 to 49 in 1959, the first rejection of a cabinet appointment since 1925. It was a rousing fight, full of complex motivations, including the desire of some senators to punish an official they considered insufficiently respectful of the Senate itself. In 1972 President Nixon's nomination of Richard Kleindienst as attorney general was on its way to an easy confirmation, despite the ideological distance between the nominee, a Goldwater conservative, and the Democratic majority, when allegations appeared in the press that a large contributor to the Republican party, International Telephone and Telegraph, had received special consideration in an antitrust prosecution by the Justice Department. Kleindienst, whose promotion from deputy attorney general had been recommended by the Senate Judiciary Committee, requested a new hearing to dispel suspicions of wrongdoing. His testimony and that of other witnesses only deepened misgivings in the Senate and in the country and induced the Senate to delay action on the nomination. But after a time the Senate lost interest in digging for facts and approved the nomination. The possibility of a major scandal was not enough to overcome the Senate's tradition of deference to the president in cabinet appointments.

Although the president normally can expect confirmation of a nomination to an independent regulatory commission, rejection may occur on ideological grounds. As a senator defending the interests of Texas, Lyndon Johnson led a successful movement to deny Leland Olds a third term on the Federal Power Commission in 1949 because, allegedly, his writings were socialistic, he had discriminated against private power and fuel companies in his decisions on the commission, and he had attempted to put an end to state authority over gas and oil production.[29]

The difference in Congress's treatment of nominations to the cabinet and other offices stems from an interest in maintaining its own preserve and allowing the president his. The legislators take control of executive and judicial patronage appointments at home and concede the higher executive appointments in Washington to the president. Their influence over domestic legislation and patronage appointments in the field allows Congress to regulate the distribution of tangible federal rewards in the home districts and stabilize its exchanges with the electorate. One reason for congressional displeasure with President Nixon's program of impounding funds for domestic programs and terminating the poverty program without legislative approval was its effect upon patronage.

When it comes to appointments to the Supreme Court, and to the regulatory commissions, which are claimed by both the executive and the legislative branches, there is continuing competition for control. The immediate goal of each branch is to prevent domination of these institutions by the other.

The preference of Congress for the status quo domestically is a function of the kind of people the members are and the way they interact in office. Disproportionately, members of Congress are small-town men (and women) of means who stayed at home while others moved about in search of opportunity. They are more sensitive to the expectations of their kind than to demands of the less privileged and the residents of the city. In Congress they gain influence as members of subject-matter committees, slowly, under a seniority system which rewards continuous service on committees, and they reach the top of the structure by serving a limited number of interests in their constituencies with appropriate legislation as committee members and by routinely trading favors with members of other committees.

The Madisonian system of separated powers and checks and balances restrains the president who tries to lead, therefore, particularly if his purpose is to press the claims of disfavored minorities—or majorities —against those of interests already heavily protected by Congress and its committees. Congress opposes redistribution and it therefore opposes important new legislation.

In foreign and military affairs, however, the relationship of the branches is reversed: the livelihood of constituents is not thought to be affected as directly, and the rewards a legislator can exchange for constituent support—patronage, pork-barrel legislation, help in processing claims with federal agencies—are also less involved. In that realm, Congress can afford to give the president a freer hand.

Abnormally Uncooperative Relations

The division of responsibility for domestic and foreign policy-making in the federal government is policed by the two branches themselves. When one branch grows overconfident and tests the defenses of the other, an angry return fire almost invariably removes the threat and reaffirms the border. A witness to this sniping could easily overestimate the seriousness of the encroachments and underestimate their conservative, corrective tendencies.

Congress and the president engaged in their most determined struggle of all from 1861 to 1868, from Lincoln's dictatorship to the impeachment and trial of Andrew Johnson. During the first weeks of his administration, as we shall later see, Lincoln directed the entry of the Union into civil war without consultation with Congress, and afterwards requested, and for the most part obtained, *ex post facto* statutory sanction for his actions. History has given Lincoln high marks for his assumption of powers to deal with a crisis inherited from his predecessor, the indecisive Buchanan, and Congress and the public gave him willing support during most of his first year in office.

But in December, 1861, reaction stirred. Dissatisfied with the pace of the war and with a union defeat near Washington, and resentful of the president's appropriation of far-reaching legislative and executive powers, Congress met to approve the establishment of a permanent joint Committee on the Conduct of the War, composed of three senators and four representatives, to share the president's power. For four years the committee was a major force in the government. With Congress behind it, the committee investigated the running of the war and the administration, summoned military leaders for cross-examination, and represented itself as the voice and conscience of the country's loyal citizens. Guided by the radicals, the Committee on the Conduct of the War was a fearless censor of the executive, sometimes right, sometimes wrong, and always a vexation for the president.[30] The president's encroachments upon Congress's preserve had at last been repudiated.

In a parallel episode in 1865, President Andrew Johnson attempted to enforce a settlement of the war upon the South by himself, as Lincoln had taken his first steps in prosecuting the war for the Union, and roused a nest of hornets in Congress. Reconstruction of the South was initiated by presidential proclamation in May of that year with the appointment of provisional governors and the promulgation of conditions of amnesty for the people of the former Confederacy, in order to revive civilian government and bring the states back into the Union. The general expectation was that presidential reconstruction was an expedient of the moment, to be followed by policies hammered out by the president and Congress together. But congressional reaction was swift and sharp. President Johnson's mild policies infuriated the radical Republicans in Congress, who retaliated with measures to assure firm federal control in the South and to protect the rights of black people from white majorities in the reconstruction legislatures. The Freedmen's Bureau Bill and the Civil Rights Bill were both passed over the veto of the president, who denounced the radicals and soon after urged the states not to ratify the proposed Fourteenth Amendment to the Constitution.

In March, 1867, Congress ended presidential reconstruction by approving legislation to establish new governments in the South, restrict the president's power as commander in chief, and prohibit the removal of civil officers without the consent of the Senate. Johnson did not take his displacement cordially. He set angrily to work to frustrate Congress's program by sabotaging the efforts of federal military commanders to keep disloyal whites from the polls. The large registration of voters which resulted promised to give existing governments control of forthcoming elections. Congress responded with a reversal of all of the president's orders, which Johnson vetoed, and on that same day both houses of Congress voted to overcome his veto. His power as president had all but vanished.[31]

Without influence and near the end of his term of office, Andrew Johnson was impeached on an array of charges bearing only a casual resemblance to the realities of his administration of the presidency, and was nearly convicted, not because he posed any further threat to congressional reconstruction, but because he was defenseless and seemed to offer Congress an opportunity to make its new ascendancy permanent by removing a balky president and demonstrating that the executive was meant to be accountable to the legislature.[32]

Friction between the president and Congress from 1861 to 1868 had the net effect of perpetuating the traditional boundaries between the branches. Lincoln set a precedent of free interpretation of the Constitution and strong leadership in moments of grave crisis; Congress set a countervailing precedent by curbing presidential prerogative after the emergency had subsided. The impeachment power was contained, ready for use in the event of serious misconduct in office, but probably never to be attempted again to settle a political dispute between the White House and the Hill.

Another story of action and reaction begins with Senator Joseph McCarthy's investigation of subversives in the executive branch in the 1950s, which led to the highest political drama of the decade. Although monitoring the administration of the laws and probing allegations of official malfeasance are orthodox enough legislative functions, the compulsion of the senator from Wisconsin was to tread harder, on more toes, than custom permitted. In 1953, after a Republican election victory in Congress that gave him a subcommittee with which to pursue his demons, McCarthy set out on investigations of supposed communist subversion in the Department of State, the information and propaganda services, and the army, with a viciousness and a flair for publicity that held the headlines until his censure the following year. His impertinent aides, Cohn and Schine, added a road show by touring American libraries overseas, ostentatiously discovering books by authors with questionable friends and ideas and using them as evidence of disloyalty in high places. Schine was soon to be drafted, whereupon the army accused the Senator of seeking preferential treatment for him and accused the private himself, wealthy scion of the hotel Schines, of attempted bribery of superior officers. Senator McCarthy retorted that the army was using Schine as a hostage in order to force an end to the investigation of communism in the army, and lashed out at the generals and at their commander in chief.[33]

The upshot was a long televised Senate hearing, McCarthy *versus* the army, superbly conducted by counsel for the army while McCarthy stormed and bullied his way to defeat. The senator's demands for internal documents to implicate the White House in the alleged conspiracy to end the probe of communist subversion were rejected by President Eisenhower. A while later McCarthy insulted some senators as well, was censured, and fell from power. While he lasted he pulled the tails of two presidents, attacked members of the executive branch from top to bottom, broke some, and frightened many others. He created the politics of his day. Eisenhower never criticized Senator McCarthy publicly, even when he impugned the loyalty of the general's old friend and brother in arms, George C. Marshall. Once at the request of local Republican leaders Eisenhower deleted a favorable reference to Marshall from a campaign speech given in Senator McCarthy's home state.

It was understandable that the president and his subordinates, reviled by a Senate investigator, should take countermeasures when it seemed safe to do so: notably the revival of the old doctrine of executive privilege, refusing key internal executive papers to legislative investigators in order to keep Congress uninformed and at bay. Congress does not always accept the invocation of executive privilege gracefully, but it usually accepts it.

Eisenhower's response was unduly slow and mild, perhaps, but it helped to restore the integrity of the executive branch and to make a repetition of McCarthyism more difficult.

President Nixon, once a congressional inquisitor himself, used the doctrine of executive privilege to keep long-range plans for foreign military assistance from falling into the hands of an unfriendly Senate Committee on Foreign Relations. When asked for the document the secretary of defense vehemently denied its existence; and then, pressed by the committee, refused to let them see it even in confidence. The committee's response was to vote an end to foreign military aid unless it received the document—or a message from the president personally invoking the privilege. President Nixon did so: "I have determined . . . that it would not be in the public interest to provide to the Congress the basic planning data on military assistance." He was concerned that "unless privacy of preliminary exchange of views between personnel of the executive branch can be maintained, the full, frank and healthy expression of opinion which is essential for the successful administration of government would be muted."[34] The outcome of the exchange was a reaffirmation of both the president's right to withhold certain potentially embarrassing information from Congress and the concern of Congress that the right not be lightly invoked by the president's subordinates.

When allegations of high-level impropriety first occurred in the Nixon administration and White House aide Peter Flanigan was invited to testify before the Senate Judiciary Committee, the president refused to allow him to go. The Senate retaliated by further postponing the vote on confirmation of Richard Kleindienst as attorney general, at least until the involvement of the president, Flanigan, and Kleindienst in the ITT antitrust affair could be clarified. Under this pressure the president reconsidered and allowed limited testimony by Flanigan, which clarified nothing but seemed to satisfy both sides as an honorable cease-fire.[35]

In his second term, when Watergate revelations began to implicate people in the White House itself, President Nixon announced a new doctrine of executive privilege, shielding all of his aides present and past from congressional inquiry. "Executive poppycock!" retorted the Senate's leading constitutional lawyer.[36] A few days later the attorney general, with presidential approval, extended executive privilege to the entire executive branch. No one in the executive might testify before Congress, he declared, if the president disapproved—a position without support in law or custom.[37] He dared Congress to attempt impeachment if it were displeased with the administration's view of privilege.

The words and demeanor of the attorney general were symptomatic of a sharp turn toward executive autocracy in the wake of the landslide election of 1972. The Nixon administration displayed open contempt for the traditional separation and balance of powers in impounding appropriated funds, dismantling the Office of Economic Opportunity without legal authorization, and conducting massive bombing in Indochina before and after the Vietnam cease-fire. Particularly evident was its contempt for Congress, which it broadly characterized as irresponsible.

Then, still another series of disclosures in the Watergate affair brought a reversal of fortunes. An administration that had seemed beyond the reach of constitutional checks, that had taunted Congress for its impotence, the public for its childlike dependency, and the press for "malicious" bias, was reduced to ignominy within a few weeks by increasing evidence of White House complicity in a campaign, transcending Watergate, to subvert the 1972 national election and to cover its tracks afterwards. When they were called to testify, the members of the White House Office came. Only at the production of certain White House tape recordings and papers did the president balk.

A related tactic of the executive to control the flow of information to congressional investigators is the appointment of principal members of the administration to the White House Office, where by tradition they are immune from questioning by legislators. President Eisenhower's right-hand man, Sherman Adams, was withheld from congressional interrogation for many years, until he was accused of influence peddling. Then the president reluctantly sent him to testify, and the testimony destroyed his public career.

Henry Kissinger's influence in foreign affairs from the sanctuary of the White House aroused congressional indignation. Before his appointment as secretary of state, Kissinger consistently declined to testify formally on Capitol Hill, and committees were obliged to settle for Secretary of State William Rogers, a man of secondary importance in the administration of foreign affairs. In this and other instances, President Nixon was accused of enhancing the authority of the White House staff in order to thwart Congress.

In the administration of President John Kennedy a very different struggle took place between the White House and the Hill over control of the Rules Committee of the House of Representatives.[38] Speaker Sam Rayburn had had trouble pushing legislation through the conservative Rules Committee, chaired by the immovable "Judge" Howard Smith of Virginia, in the Democratic-controlled Congress before Kennedy's election. Then, a net loss of liberal Democrats in Congress in the same election that brought a liberal Democrat to the White House made it likely that Congress would be asked to do more and, checked by a conservative coalition of Republicans and southern Democrats, would in fact do less. Under the circumstances the presence of a committee with the power to block the few measures that might survive other tests was galling. The president's answer to the threat was to pack the Rules Committee with liberals, with the help of Rayburn. Kennedy had already made his move to bring the Senate into line by selecting Lyndon Johnson, a capable but willful majority leader, as his running mate, allowing the less talented and less combative Mike Mansfield to move up to the top post.[39]

Presidential tinkering with committee membership and other internal affairs of Congress is fraught with risk. Kennedy made perfunctory efforts to play down his own part in the packing—to a question in a press conference he replied that he was only a bystander, "an interested citizen," and the reporters chuckled—but his prestige was at stake. He launched a full presidential patronage campaign to build a coalition of Democrats and Republicans for the assault. Rayburn threatened to remove a senior member of the committee who had crossed party lines to support Richard Nixon in the presidential election if he and his colleagues did not consent to the packing. Few opportunities to persuade were missed, and the final vote was once postponed in order to make certain that the greatest possible number of Kennedy's supporters were in town to vote.

The vote was a close 217 to 212 in favor of enlarging the committee. Liberals were appointed, and for a while the bottleneck seemed to be broken. Then Congress reacted. Judge Smith refused to provide additional chairs at the committee table for the new members, until constituents of one sent a splendid padded chair for their man and threatened to upset the committee's delicate status system. More importantly, the lingering resentment of a young president who had won a battle on foreign territory probably stiffened the resistance of the House to subsequent White House requests. Neutralizing the Rules Committee, as it turned out, did not do the president much good. In his three years in office he was notably weak as a legislative leader. Presidents may now hesitate before intervening so boldly in committee affairs.

In 1965 there was another case of failure to upset the customary division of authority between Congress and the White House: the struggle over closing military bases in the United States. Because bases have both military and patronage implications, presidents had traditionally been careful to consult with friendly legislators before deciding when and where to order closings within the fifty states. It is one of the few aspects of military affairs in which Congress shows intense interest. But when Secretary of Defense Robert McNamara shrugged off patronage considerations in his resolute pursuit of efficiency and economy in the Pentagon, Congress responded with corrective legislation. It added a provision to a military construction act requiring the executive to submit plans for the closing of military installations to Congress between January 1 and April 30 each year, and to close no installation until Congress had had 120 days to consider the matter. If Congress adjourned within this period, the plans were to be submitted anew at the next session. The plain purpose of the provision was to allow influential members of Congress time to build pressure against base closings and, if necessary, to persuade the president to overrule his secretary.

President Johnson vetoed the measure. It was "repugnant to the Constitution," he said, a "fundamental encroachment" of the legislature on executive authority, certain to affect the management of the military services adversely. But he went on to say that he would accept a compromise bill with a "reasonable reporting provision." Congress complied with a revised version specifying a thirty-day waiting period and the crisis was over.[40] The status quo was restored.

President Nixon traded blows with Congress on the issue of appointments to the Supreme Court. In rejecting his nominations of Clement Haynsworth and G. Harrold Carswell to the Court, the Senate dealt the president a grievous defeat. Its reasons were mixed: a wish to embarrass the president; distress over the impending change in the Court from liberalism to conservatism; the revelations of ethical insensitivity and racism in the records of Haynsworth and Carswell, respectively; and the caliber of the nominees apart from ideology. Unquestionably there were conservatives favoring confirmation who were concerned about ideology to the exclusion of considerations of competence and morals, just as there were a good number of liberal senators who were delighted to find nonideological grounds for voting against confirmation.

President Nixon characterized the votes against his nominees as an assault upon presidential authority. In a letter to a Republican senator the president said, "What is centrally at issue . . . is the constitutional responsibility of the president to appoint members of the Court—and whether this responsibility can be frustrated by those who wish to substitute their own philosophy or their own subjective judgment for that of the one person entrusted by the Constitution with the power of appointment. . . . If the Senate attempts to substitute its judgment as to who should be appointed, the traditional constitutional balance is in jeopardy. . . ." Senators reacted bitterly to an interpretation of the Constitution that reduced the power of advice and consent to nothing.

And after it was all over, the president went on television to assail his antagonists.

> I have reluctantly concluded—with the Senate presently constituted— I cannot successfully nominate to the Supreme Court any federal appellate judge from the South who believes as I do in the strict construction of the Constitution. Judges Carswell and Haynsworth have endured with admirable dignity vicious assaults on their intelligence, their honesty, and their character. They have been falsely charged with being racist, but when all the hypocrisy is stripped away, the real issue was their philosophy of strict construction of the Constitution—a philosophy that I share —and the fact that they had the misfortune of being born in the South.[41]

Some time later the president struck at the Senate again, and at the Supreme Court, by giving active consideration to a number of clearly unqualified men and women for appointment to the Court, among them Senator Robert Byrd. It was supposed that the president anticipated automatic support in the Senate for one of their own, despite the senator's unattractiveness, and that he wished to rub the senators' noses collectively in the mess they had dropped on his doorstep. Outrage among the public and members of the legal profession caused the president to substitute the name of an eminently qualified southern conservative, Lewis Powell, whose easy confirmation restored the equilibrium of the two branches.

Our several examples of conflict between the president and Congress describe a pattern: blows are traded but typically the outcome is a reaffirmation of old roles. President and Congress continue to repel attacks and enjoy separate spheres of influence.

Abnormal Cooperation— Legislative Passivity

The two branches have come together fully in domestic policy-making a few times in our history. They are remembered as moments of crisis and presidential greatness, when the president assumed national leadership and Congress suspended its negativism for a while. Two forms of cooperation have occurred in the American experience: presidential autocracy, with a passive Congress either approving the actions of the President *ex post facto* or delegating sweeping legislative authority in advance, and legislative leadership, in flurries of intense legislative activity directed and supported by the president.

The only pure example of presidential autocracy in domestic affairs is Abraham Lincoln's early war leadership, and it is also the only instance in the history of the republic in which civil war obliterated the distinction between war and internal affairs. Lincoln postponed a scheduled meeting of Congress when he took office and ran the war single-handedly—and ran the country, too, to the extent that it was affected by his war policies. His constitutionally questionable actions in this period included calling forth the militia of the several states, asking for three-year volunteers for the army, proclaiming a blockade of southern ports, increasing the size of the regular army and navy, suspending the writ of habeas corpus to permit the detention of suspects without recourse to the courts, and spending money without congressional appropriation.

When Congress convened on July 4, 1861, the president sent a message describing the events of the war and his steps "to carry out the war power of the government." He asked for the members' approval. "Must a government, of necessity, be too strong for the liberties of its own people," he wondered, "or too weak to maintain its own existence?" More important than the specific demands of the Constitution, in his view, was the ultimate responsibility of the government to preserve itself. He went on to ask for money and troops, and, to the applause of Congress as the message was read, for "the legal means for making this contest a short and decisive one."

Congress responded generously. His appointments were confirmed by the Senate. An army of 500,000 men was provided, a full 100,000 more than he had requested. He was given wide powers to put down insurrections, to close ports, and to demand loyalty oaths of federal employees. And then on August 6, Congress legalized his doubtful acts by means of a rider in a military pay bill. The blockade and the suspension of habeas corpus, however, were omitted.

> Be it enacted by the Senate and House of Representatives of the United States of America, . . . That all the acts, proclamations, and orders of the president of the United States after the fourth of March, eighteen hundred and sixty-one, respecting the army and navy of the United States, are hereby approved and in all respects legalized and made valid, to the same intent and with the same effect as if they had been issued and done under the previous and express authority and direction of the Congress of the United States.[42]

Two years later Congress authorized the president to suspend the writ of habeas corpus during the period of the rebellion, and the Supreme Court affirmed the power of the president to proclaim a naval blockade in the *Prize Cases*.[43] By this time, as we have noted, the early spirit of cooperation had degenerated into mistrust. The Committee on the Conduct of the War had been at work for a year and a half. The following year, in the electoral campaign of 1864, the leaders of Lincoln's own party in the two houses of Congress issued a manifesto asserting that "the authority of Congress is paramount." No longer inclined to countenance executive autocracy, they warned the president that "if he wishes our support he must confine himself to his executive duties—to obey and to execute, not to make laws." Executive authority was to suffer in the years ahead, but Lincoln had set a memorable precedent that a president, as the responsible agent of government in time of crisis, might transcend the limits imposed by the Constitution on the exercise of power. It was to Lincoln's credit that he employed his great authority with restraint and candor.

In World War I, Woodrow Wilson had even more power, most of it by act of Congress before rather than after the fact.[44] He acted on his own when it seemed necessary, arming merchant ships in 1917 when the Senate was mired in a filibuster, imposing wartime censorship, and establishing a number of executive agencies. But Wilson was more effective with legislators than Lincoln had been, and he secured the greater part of his authority in the form of broad statutory delegation. The Lever Act of 1917 in particular contained grants of authority to the president to make rules and regulations for the war economy, including price-fixing and the seizure of industries.[45] He also induced Congress not to establish a Committee on the Conduct of the War.

In World War II the distribution of power was similar. As a strong president who would act alone if Congress refused its cooperation, Roosevelt enjoyed a full measure of delegated authority and little congressional interference with his conduct of the war. His questionable order for the relocation of Japanese-Americans from the West Coast was ratified by Congress. In 1942 he demanded price controls of Congress.

> I ask the Congress to take this action by the first of October. Inaction on your part by that date will leave me with an inescapable responsibility to the people of this country to see to it that the war effort is no longer imperiled by threat of economic chaos.
>
> In the event that Congress should fail to act, and act adequately, I shall accept the responsibility, and I will act. ...
>
> When the war is won, the powers under which I act automatically revert to the People—to whom they belong.[46]

A Special War Investigations Committee chaired by Senator Harry Truman remained cooperative and was in no sense a revival of the Committee on the Conduct of the War of the Lincoln era.

Putting the precedent together, the burden of the American tradition is not independent action or cooperation with Congress in time of emergency, nor is it delegation before the fact or after the fact. It is the discretion a president enjoys to choose among these alternatives when the time comes. In Great Britain it is very different. Parliament delegates extraordinary emergency authority to the cabinet; in effect it hands over the lawmaking power to the executive for the duration of the crisis. The cabinet acquires bipartisan membership and parliamentary elections are suspended. As in Lincoln's war administration, the government's powers over civilians are exercised with restraint—the traditional rights of individuals are respected as fully as possible. Under the Defence of the Realm Acts of World Wars I and II, the writ of habeas corpus was suspended, for example, but few were detained without trial; military trials were authorized for civilians, but rarely used.[47]

The favorable experience of the British, however, does not prove that broad delegation is a universal solution. In Canada, Prime Minister Trudeau invoked the War Measures Act, similar to Britain's wartime enabling acts, to deal with the threat of terrorism by French-speaking separatists in 1970. Under the act suspicious persons could be arrested without warrant by police or soldiers and held for as long as three weeks without formal charge or the opportunity of bail, and punishment of five years in jail was provided for any who assisted, or were members of, proscribed organizations. The government made broad use of its extraordinary powers, curtailing the rights of expression and association, searching and arresting freely, in its efforts to curb civil strife. In the aftermath, opinion in Canada was well divided as to whether Mr. Trudeau had acted prudently or with insufficient regard for the rights of the people.

The lesson of the Weimar Republic is less equivocal. Article 48 of the German Constitution allowed the president to suspend rights and assume control of the armed forces; enabling acts not unlike Britain's suspended civil liberties and delegated legislative authority to the executive by a two-thirds vote of the legislature. Repeated employment of these powers by democratic leaders in the 1920s and early 1930s provided precedent for their use as a facade for the assumption of absolute power by Adolf Hitler in 1933 and the destruction of democracy in Germany.

There is, in short, no reason to consider enabling acts inherently superior to the *ad hoc* devices of crisis government in the American political system.

Abnormal Cooperation— Legislative Partnership

When Congress sees a profit in cooperation with the White House, it prefers partnership to passivity. The prime examples of productive exchange between president and Congress in domestic affairs are Woodrow Wilson's New Freedom, Franklin Roosevelt's New Deal, and Lyndon Johnson's Great Society.

Wilson was the first president to mobilize all of the resources of his office in support of a legislative program. He collaborated with the leaders of Congress on one bill at a time, fighting when necessary, and appealing to public opinion—when his tariff bill was in trouble he blamed the lobbies and asked for public support. In a year and a half, with inexhaustible drive and finesse, he had maneuvered through Congress, in addition to tariff reform, the Federal Reserve Act, the Clayton Antitrust Act, the Fair Trade Act, and the Smith-Lever Act establishing an agricultural extension system. Remarkably his work as a domestic reformer continued off and on again for the rest of his term of office.[48] No other president has enjoyed such prolonged success in his relations with Congress.

In his first hundred days, Franklin Roosevelt supervised the passage of a prodigious array of legislation, with less forethought and intellectual consistency than Wilson, but with more charm, a politic adaptability, and the impetus of a serious economic depression, in which a fourth of the labor force was unemployed, national income was down by half, and state and local welfare programs were failing. He acted quickly, calling Congress into session and proclaiming a bank holiday to stem a run on the banks by frightened depositors. When Congress met, it "approved and confirmed" the president's actions in an Emergency Banking Act and put to rest any question of the lawfulness of Roosevelt's invocation of the broad emergency powers of the wartime Trading with the Enemy Act for peacetime purposes. Congress was so willing to follow the President's lead that it debated and passed the act and sent it to the White House in one working day.

There followed fourteen weeks more of legislative ferment, producing an Economy Act, the Civilian Conservation Corps, the Tennessee Valley Authority, loans to state banks, the establishment of a United States Employment Service, the abandonment of the gold standard, the Federal Emergency Relief Act, the Agricultural Adjustment Act, the Emergency Farm Mortgage Act, the Truth-in-Securities Act, another banking act initiating a system of deposit guarantees, the Home Owners Loan Act, the National Industrial Recovery Act, the Railroad Coordination Act, the Farm Credit Act, and more. Many of the acts were presidential in origin and purpose, a few were the progeny of legislators, brought to life with White House aid, and some such as the National Industrial Recovery Act were genuinely collaborative—even when it is the president who takes the credit, a bill may stem from measures under consideration on the Hill for months or years beforehand.[49]

Roosevelt's effectiveness as a partner of the legislature waned after the Hundred Days. Despite his return by a record margin in the election of 1936, he could urge very little upon Congress. His court-packing bill ran aground in the Senate, his attempted purge of anti-New Deal Democrats in Congress failed in 1938, and with the sole exception of the Fair Labor Standards Act in 1938, his last eight years in office were barren of significant domestic enactments. Even in death he won no legislative favor. Congress proposed a constitutional amendment in 1947 to limit the president to two terms in office, perhaps to improve the workings of democracy, but certainly to censure Roosevelt posthumously for overshadowing the balance of the federal government for over twelve years.

The generation between the early New Deal and the next flurry of legislation in the Johnson administration was marked by only one additional piece of legislation of domestic importance, the Taft-Hartley Act of 1947, which was passed over the veto of the president. Congress gave Harry Truman a large raise and a tax-free expense account in lieu of domestic legislation.

Lyndon Johnson's Great Society was largely a refurbishing and re-packaging of ideas that had been in circulation for years. But success as a legislative leader is less a matter of originality than of fashioning a workable program from the thoughts of others and building a coalition to support it in Washington and in the country. The War on Poverty, one of Johnson's first important accomplishments, was a mélange of ideas from the Council of Economic Advisors, agency proposals strung together by the Bureau of the Budget, legislative ideas still in Congress from the Kennedy administration, a nostrum or two from the New Deal, and suggestions of task forces, a presidential study commission, and a few unattached intellectuals. Also in his first year President Johnson engineered the passage of the Civil Rights Act of 1964, for all its compromises the broadest and toughest civil rights law ever enacted by Congress. In 1965 with a new, more liberal Congress, President Johnson requested and received legislation on medical care for the aged, aid to primary and secondary schools, immigration reform, voting rights, excise tax reduction, and aid to urban areas, to mention only the most noteworthy. As in the Roosevelt administration, relations cooled before long, but the new laws had lasting effects. Lyndon Johnson may be remembered mainly for his part in the war in Indochina and counted among the ordinary presidents, but as a domestic reformer he was a rare success.

To lead Congress in domestic innovation, a president must convince the members that they have more to gain than to lose from engaging in exchanges with him. It takes a capable president and a progressive or liberal legislature to begin with, and an aroused public to make the representatives and senators willing to court the favor of new, broader interests in the constituencies. In the absence of these conditions, which recur infrequently, the most a president can do is gain a measure of popularity by berating Congress for its inactivity.

The Parliamentary Alternative

The American system of government with its Madisonian tensions and uncertainties in the relations of the executive and the legislature has sometimes been compared unfavorably with cabinet government and the parliamentary system. As noted at the time of the Watergate disclosures, a parliamentary structure allows the replacement of an executive which has lost the confidence of the people's representatives, after new elections if necessary. Also the American form appears less democratic: in foreign and more particularly military affairs the president is not effectively checked by the people's representatives in Congress, and in domestic affairs the president and Congress are typically deadlocked. But in a parliamentary government such as the British, the executive and the legislature are tied together in mutual dependency: they cooperate or they step aside and let others try. Americans who favor a positive linkage of executive demand and legislative response find the parliamentary alternative attractive.

Now and then, in a spirit of compromise, someone suggests grafting parts of the parliamentary plan to the American system of presidential government. In 1864 Congressman George Pendleton proposed that cabinet members be given seats in the House of Representatives with the privilege of entering into debate and the responsibility of being present on certain days each month to answer questions. It was a time when the Committee on the Conduct of the War, in its own way, was bringing Congress and the executive branch closer together. The plan was embodied in a bill introduced by Representative J. D. Long in 1886 and later revived by President William Howard Taft.[50] Taft believed the president's leadership of Congress would be enhanced by the change. In 1963 the Senate passed a resolution to allow *former* presidents to participate in the affairs of the chamber and its committees —without vote and without expectation that relations between the branches would be materially affected, or even that the invitation would be accepted.[51]

It is interesting to compare the views of two Englishmen, Harold Laski and Herman Finer, who both lived in the United States, wrote perceptively on the American political system, and differed profoundly on the ability of British institutions to survive a crossing of the Atlantic. Laski feared that parliamentary reforms would work mischief: they would turn members of the cabinet into rivals of the president for the favor of Congress, he thought, saddle the president with men of divided loyalties who would be too influential to dismiss, and in the long run weaken the presidency vis-à-vis Congress.[52]

Finer's proposal for improving the government of separated powers with parliamentary reforms was to create a cabinet of eleven vice-presidents to share the president's authority, all twelve to be nominated together in national party conventions and elected for four years along with a Congress with terms modified to match. Under Finer's plan the president would have the right to dismiss members of the cabinet and to name a line of succession among them. Linkage with Congress would be assured by two requirements: that the president and each of his vice-presidents be members of the House or Senate at the time of their election, or have served at least four years in Congress in the past; and that they sit in the House of Representatives, where they would face the losing slate of candidates, who would be given seats and the duty of leading the oppositon. The president and the cabinet would have the right to resign if they were thwarted by Congress and to force new four-year elections for everyone. The two branches of government would be bridged, in short, by the common training, associations, electoral mandate, and tenure of Congress and the cabinet.[53]

British institutions are unlikely to be borrowed for use in the United States, it is safe to say. The last full consideration, and firm rejection, of outright fusion of executive and legislative powers took place in the Philadelphia Convention of 1787, where both the Virginia and the New Jersey Plans contemplated election of the executive by Congress. But Finer's ideas lend perspective and a sense of what might have been had American institutions not diverged from the British in the last two hundred years.

Even within the framework of the Constitution, institutions of a more parliamentary turn might have evolved with a nudge or two. The impeachment power could have been used to hold the president closely accountable to Congress on pain of removal from office. It seemed about to be put to that purpose in 1868, only to fail by a margin of one vote in the Senate. Although it was argued that recent presidents committed "high crimes and misdemeanors" in directing the war in Indochina —war crimes, crimes against peace, and crimes against humanity under the Nuermberg Principles—there was never a likelihood of impeachment.[54] In the Watergate era, impeachment was not even seriously discussed in Congress until the evidence of scandal was overwhelming. It is hard to believe, therefore, that impeachment and conviction could occur in more commonplace circumstances, as a regular part of the system. Similarly the election of the president as conceived by the Philadelphia Convention was to have been the responsibility of the House of Representatives upon the nomination of the electoral college, normally, but the unanticipated appearance of a two-party system to focus the voting in the several states made a run-off election in the House, for want of a majority in the college, the exception rather than the rule. These and other devices might have made the president a creature of Congress.

It was within the two-party system, however, that the Democrats under the determined leadership of Woodrow Wilson, brought the two branches closer than ever. More than any other President, Wilson admired British political practices. As a student he had advocated a form of cabinet government for the United States.

Let ... the leaders of the parties be made responsible. ... This can be done by making the leaders of the dominant party in Congress the executive officers of the legislative will; by making them also members of the

president's cabinet, and thus at once the executive chiefs of the departments . . . and the leaders of their party on the floor of Congress; in a word,
by having done with the standing committees, and constituting the cabinet advisors both of the president and Congress.[55]

But with the passage of time, and the example of stronger chief
executives than he had witnessed earlier, Wilson turned to presidential
leadership through a strong party organization as the way to draw the
forces of government together, and acted on his beliefs when he took
office.

Lesser presidents—most presidents—have lacked the wit to use the
lessons of the past and of the rest of the democratic world to mold the
office to their will. Wilson exploited the office of president successfully
because he was a flexible, inventive bargainer during most of his years
in the White House. When he abandoned compromise and exchange for
unyielding zero-sum winner-take-all relations with the Senate at the
end of his administration, he failed.

Notes

[1]Richard Harris, *Decision* (New York: Ballantine Books, Inc., 1972), pp.
106–7, 139–40.

[2]Tom Wicker, *JFK and LBJ* (Baltimore: Penguin Books Inc., 1969), Part I.

[3]James Sterling Young, *The Washington Community: 1800–1825* (New
York: Columbia University Press, 1966), pp. 157–210.

[4]Theodore Roosevelt, *An Autobiography* (New York: The Macmillan Company, 1964), p. 372.

[5]William Howard Taft, *Our Chief Magistrate and His Powers* (New York:
Columbia University Press, 1925), pp. 138–39.

[6]Arthur W. Macmahon, "Wilson: Political Leader and Administrator," in
The Philosophy and Policies of Woodrow Wilson, ed. Earl Lathem (Chicago:
University of Chicago Press, 1958), Chap. 6.

[7]*Congressional Quarterly,* July 23, 1965, pp. 1434–36.

[8]*New York Times,* November 21, 1969, p. 20.

[9]Harris, *Decision,* pp. 105–6, 154, 161, 210–11.

[10]*New York Times,* March 6, 1973, p. 20.

[11]*Congressional Quarterly,* February 26, 1972, pp. 443–45.

[12]*New York Times,* April 3, 1973, p. 28.

[13]Carlton Jackson, *Presidential Vetoes* (Athens: University of Georgia Press,
1967), p. 205.

[14]This passage is drawn from James M. Burns, *Roosevelt: The Soldier of
Freedom* (New York: Harcourt Brace Jovanovich, Inc., 1970), pp. 434–37.

[15]U.S., *Congressional Record,* 86th Cong., 2d sess., 1960, CVI, Part 2, 711.

[16]Wicker, *JFK and LBJ,* Part I; Arthur M. Schlesinger, Jr., *A Thousand Days* (Boston: Houghton Mifflin Company, 1965), Chap. 36, Sec. 4; Theodore Sorensen, *Kennedy* (New York: Harper & Row, Publishers, 1966), pp. 342ff; James L. Sundquist, *Politics and Policy: The Eisenhower, Kennedy and Johnson Years* (Washington, D.C.: The Brookings Institution, 1968), pp. 478–80.

[17]*Congressional Quarterly,* February 19, 1972, p. 386.

[18]Schlesinger, *A Thousand Days,* pp. 707–8.

[19]*New York Times,* January 23, 1971, p. 8; *Congressional Quarterly,* June 25, 1971, p. 1362.

[20]*Congressional Quarterly,* June 25, 1971, p. 1362; September 25, 1971, p. 1973 December 18, 1971, p. 2587; *Albuquerque Journal,* November 18, 1971.

[21]*New York Times,* April 16, 1972, Sec. 4, p. 1.

[22]The words are Lyndon Johnson's. *New York Times,* July 11, 1966, p. 1; *Congressional Quarterly,* July 8, 1966, pp. 1441–42.

[23]Francis D. Wormuth, *The Vietnam War: The President versus the Constitution,* an occasional paper of the Center for the Study of Democratic Institutions, 1968, passim.

[24]*Congress and the Nation* (Washington, D.C.: Congressional Quarterly Service, 1969), II, 629.

[25]Henry Steele Commager, "Can We Limit Presidential Power?" *New Republic,* April 6, 1968, p. 15.

[26]*Ibid.,* pp. 15–18.

[27]*Congressional Quarterly Almanac,* 1969, p. 999.

[28]E.g., U.S., *Congressional Record,* 82nd Cong., 2d sess., 1952, XCVIII, Part 1, 908.

[29]*Congress and the Nation* (Washington, D.C.: Congressional Quarterly Service, 1965), p. 105a.

[30]John G. Nicolay and John Hay, *Abraham Lincoln* (New York: Century, 1914), V, 150–51.

[31]Eric L. McKitrick, *Andrew Johnson and Reconstruction* (Chicago: University of Chicago Press, 1960), pp. 4–13, 488–94.

[32]*Ibid.,* pp. 486ff.

[33]*Congress and the Nation,* pp. 1718ff.

[34]*New York Times,* September 1, 1971, p. 1.

[35]E.g., *New York Times,* March 3, 1971, p. 3.

[36]*New York Times,* April 3, 1973, p. 28.

[37]*New York Times,* April 11, 1973, p. 1.

[38]Wicker, *JFK* and *LBJ,* Part I.

[39]*New York Times,* August 3, 1970, p. 1.

[40]*Congress and the Nation,* II, 93a–94a.

[41]*New York Times,* April 10, 1970, p. 14.

[42]12 Stat. 326 (1861).

[43]12 Stat. 755 (1863); *The Prize Cases,* 2 Bl. 635 (1863).

[44]Clinton Rossiter, *Constitutional Dictatorship* (Princeton: Princeton University Press, 1948), Chaps. 16, 18.

[45]40 Stat. 276 (1917).

[46]U.S., *Congressional Record,* 77th Cong., 2d sess., 1942, LXXXVIII, Part 5, 7044.

[47]Rossiter, *Constitutional Dictatorship,* Chaps. 11, 14.

[48]Macmahon, "Wilson," pp. 107–12.

[49]Lawrence H. Chamberlain, "The President, Congress, and Legislation, *Political Science Quarterly,* LXI, No. 1 (1946), 47–49.

[50]Harold J. Laski, *The American Presidency* (New York: Harper & Brothers Publishers, 1940), pp. 96–97.

[51]*Congress and the Nation,* p. 1438.

[52]Laski, *The American Presidency,* pp. 100–105.

[53]Herman Finer, *The Presidency; Crisis and Regeneration* (Chicago: University of Chicago Press, 1960), pp. 302ff.

[54]*New Republic,* May 1, 1971, pp. 13–14.

[55]Woodrow Wilson, "Committee or Cabinet Government?" in *The Public Papers of Woodrow Wilson,* eds. Ray Stannard Baker and W. E. Dodds (New York: Harper & Brothers Publishers, 1925), I, 112.

The President and the Public

Because the president needs a steady flow of public support and the public requires presidential authority and leadership, the normal exchange between the two is warm and vital. It is a twofold exchange, political and psychological, and is largely free of the traditions of competition and suspicion which encumber the president's relations with Congress and other parts of the government. The strains of election and reelection apart, the president and the public usually give one another comfort and support. Of the two sides of the exchange, the political is obvious and straightforward; the psychological is not.

Popular Support of the President

To enact and administer his programs the president needs the weight of public opinion on Congress and to some extent on the bureaucracy and the courts. The government over which he presides is divided by a Constitution designed to restrain the exercise of power and by Congress's delegation of authority over policy-making to its own committees, to autonomous regulatory agencies, and to state and local governments. Amending the rules and rewards in a forest of entrenched political interests exercising delegated power is so difficult that the president must exaggerate the seriousness of public problems and the efficacy of his solutions—must oversell—in the hope of bringing public opinion to his side and overcoming the inertia of the system. The public has the power to support the president or let him founder. A president who attempted massive social change without stirring up the public for a war on this or a crusade against that would be likely to fail in the diffuse American political system.[1]

The typical president also needs a more general kind of public support: popularity, perhaps adulation, in pursuit of an end no more abstruse than his own sense of well-being. Today public opinion polls provide a fever chart of responses to stock questions on approval or disapproval of the way the president is handling his job, month by month, year by year, which are read as avidly by presidents themselves as by the public. Lyndon Johnson retained a private polling firm to send him regular reports and assigned an aide to monitor other polls.[2] But before there were polls, presidents sought the warmth and approval of crowds for personal tribute as well as for specific political purposes. For all their differences, Theodore Roosevelt and Woodrow Wilson, the cowboy and the schoolmaster, were alike in their dependence upon the love and respect of the masses, which Roosevelt courted with brave deeds, costumes, and theatrics, and with the writing and speaking that were Wilson's forte too. Both were more disposed than their predecessors to cultivate the favor of the press and to engage in public speaking as a regular function of the presidency. They were strong presidents, yet it is interesting that as youngsters they were particularly slow, inept, and sickly. Each made a career of self-improvement, without any lasting satisfaction in his accomplishments, and sought the affection of the masses as a reassurance of his worth and acceptability. In Wilson's case the respect of the public at large was in some measure a substitute for the affection of individual men and women. He was lonely as a child and lonely as an adult. As president he was suspicious of people he encountered. Friendships soured. And when he failed to come to terms with fellow politicians or heads of state he appealed to "the people," in the abstract, as the supreme authority.

Contrasting the undoubted strength of these presidents, or of Lyndon Johnson more recently, with their vanity and their stratagems for bracing sagging self-esteem, we can see great weakness and great strength of character linked together in some of our presidents. An awareness of early deficiencies, real and imagined, could be appeased by real accomplishments, but in these talented, compulsively ambitious men self-doubts and insecurities remained. In James David Barber's classification, presidents of this kind are identified by their active approach to office (they try hard) and their "negative affect" (they have little pleasure in the effort). Other presidents are active with positive affect (Truman, for example, an energetic chief executive who enjoyed the responsibility of office); passive with negative affect (Coolidge, who found the little he did in office onerous); or passive with positive affect (Harding, a genial man without much idea of what to do as president). A Harding as president also seeks popular acclaim, but more on the order of applause and friendly smiles than the respect and esteem for which strong, compulsive presidents hunger.[3]

Unfortunately for the peace of mind of the presidents who value popular esteem, the people are fickle; they have rhythms of affirmation and denial which weigh on the White House and influence the ebb and flow of presidential popularity. Three patterns stand out: the massive veto, the honeymoon, and the crisis syndrome.

Walter Lippmann has decried the tendency of public opinion to impose a veto on the government in crucial periods of decision.[4] Sometimes the public is apathetic, he writes; at other times it rouses itself and utters a resounding No! It is the way a mass speaks and it is, in Lippmann's judgment, "destructively wrong at the critical junctures." When it is vital to arm, to intervene in a developing conflict, to withdraw from an area of conflict, or to negotiate a compromise peace, the public is likely to disapprove a change in the course of government policy, "a morbid derangement of the functions of power." One may note that when a massive public veto was imposed upon official United States policy for Vietnam years later, Lippmann approved.

Presidents enjoy a honeymoon of relatively high popularity during their first months in office, followed by a fairly steady decline of about 5 percent annually in the public polls. Even the strong presidents who are remembered for their legislation—Franklin Roosevelt and Lyndon Johnson above all others in this century—made their mark in a brief period of leadership succeeded by years of disappointment. Dwight Eisenhower was an exception to the rule. A man of great personal appeal who chose not to put himself to the test of legislative leadership, he became more popular as the years passed. Presidents who promote programs tend to alienate one group after another as they serve their time in office and steadily incur net losses in the opinion polls.[5] How far a president will go to alienate no one, and to remain all things to all people, is evident in the remarks of President Nixon in the aftermath of a performance of *No, No, Nanette* in New York.

> My wife and I of course like musical comedy. We like the theater also. I don't mean by that that they should always be old musicals. But I think that this musical that they call escapist—I don't look at it that way. I think that after a long day, most of us need a lift in the evening. I don't mean by that that sometimes I don't want to go see a very serious play or something of that sort. . . .[6]

A third rhythm is the tendency of public opinion to rally in support of the president in time of international crisis, no matter who starts it and who wins. President Kennedy's popularity rose significantly as a result of both the Bay of Pigs and the Cuban Missile crisis, though one was a patent disaster and the other widely regarded in this country as a signal victory. The lesson of the crisis syndrome, which presidents have been slow to appreciate, is that one can manipulate public opinion by manufacturing crises. The secret Pentagon Papers demonstrated what critics of President Johnson's Vietnam policy had long contended, that the Gulf of Tonkin incident, the alleged firing by the North Vietnamese on United States naval vessels, was a manufactured crisis. The Pentagon had been looking for an excuse to widen the war, and whether the Gulf of Tonkin incident was faked, provoked, or merely embraced by the United States is of secondary importance. President Nixon's series of summit conferences in the election year of 1972, culminating in the meeting in Peking, is another instance of crisis manipulation. Experience indicates that presidents benefit from sudden military interventions; major developments in ongoing wars; major diplomatic developments, including summit conferences with traditional enemies; and technological breakthroughs on the order of Sputnik. Wars, though, have the opposite effect on presidential popularity, as Harry Truman and Lyndon Johnson discovered. Nor are personal crises helpful—neither the attempted assassination of President Truman nor Eisenhower's heart attack caused a surge in popularity as measured by the polls.[7]

In their quest for support, presidents have both personal and institutional tools at their disposal for informing, appeasing, or hoodwinking the public. Some presidents are abler and more daring than others. In theory all must reckon with Lincoln's rule that you can't fool all of the people all of the time. Lyndon Johnson and Richard Nixon led a good many people to believe they were trying, however, and the result was a credibility gap during the war in Vietnam, renewed in the Watergate period. But as long as there is some balance between a president's desire to misinform and to inform, he has a ready audience.

Presidential Communication with the People

In the early days of the Republic, local politics were as likely to capture the interest of the public as more remote and abstract national affairs. But today the press, including television and radio, is able to bring national and world figures into the home and displace local and state news. An inversion of geographical and political distances has occurred, to the benefit of the presidency, although the ability of presidents to make good use of the potential of the media varies.

There have been masters of English prose in the White House, Lincoln and Wilson outstanding among them, who had both the talent with language and the finesse to apply their talent with purpose and effect in different settings. Lincoln could be folksy or Olympian. Wilson could move from deft analytical prose to crowd-pleasing platitudes as the occasion required. For men such as Andrew Johnson and Richard Nixon, each a stylist in bathos and belligerence, speechmaking was a cathartic, a joyful release of accumulated tensions. Nixon's Checkers Speech, in which he defended himself against allegations of financial wrong-doing with a family melodrama of trivia from the misstatement that his wife was born on St. Patrick's day to the story of the gift dog, Checkers, and assured his continuance on the 1952 national ticket with General Eisenhower, will surely be remembered along with George Washington's Farewell Address to the nation and Lincoln's Gettysburg Address as an American political classic—on the basis of popular acclaim if not as the critics' choice. Both Nixon and Andrew Johnson affected an iron self-control in ordinary public appearances, but now and then lashed out in lapses that revealed underlying frustrations.

Last are those without talent in the language who get along with other skills. Warren Harding, a disastrous president, and Dwight Eisenhower, a more ordinary one, substituted pomposity and verbal disarray, respectively, for communication. A sample of Harding:

> Service is the supreme commitment of life. I would rejoice to acclaim the era of the golden rule and crown it with the autocracy of service. . . . I have taken the solemn oath of office on that passage of holy writ wherein it is asked: "What doth the Lord require of thee but to do justly and to love mercy and walk humbly with thy God?" This I plight to God and country.[8]

Eisenhower's unrehearsed language was an inimitable mixture of moral fervor and plain confusion. Witness these exchanges from a typical news conference:

This morning, or maybe it was yesterday, hearings were starting again for a mutual security program. I don't want to take up too much of your time for the simple reason that everyone here has heard expressed time and again my views about mutual security, its need for real support if we are concerned about our nation's security, and our nation's position in the international world. And, I repeat, it is not a partisan question; it's one of those things that should be discussed and debated on the basis of need and logic and of good sense and fact, and not considered at all in any partisan attitude. I should repeat that you people know the dependence that I place upon it in assuring the security of the United States, and as a tool in our battle for a lessening of tensions and some advancement toward peace.

Any questions?

Question: Mr. President, ... some Senators feel that you are taking too timid an approach in your request for the Mutual Security Program, and also that you are spending too much on military foreign aid and not enough on economic.

The President: Well, with respect to this timid approach, I think I am correct, although I am speaking only from memory, and if I have to correct my statement I shall do so at my next meeting with you, I think that each time I have made recommendations on mutual security it has been cut down by the Congress. I therefore think that it has not been carried forward as vigorously as it should be. ...

Question: Well, Mr. President, however, there has been considerable criticism that we have not been too wise in allocating military aid to, for instance, Pakistan. That aid is regarded by India as something hostile, and ... India felt it necessary to buy arms herself to counter the arms we are giving to Pakistan.

The President: I want to tell you that such questions that you are now raising have been studied with the—by hours and weeks and months, literally, by this government, this administration, and calling in often people, legislative leaders of both parties, in the effort to get a reasonable and, as nearly as possible, correct answer about this whole thing. Of course there is criticism. Everybody in this field has his own particular beliefs. But I say this: so far as I know, there has been nothing that is done here except on the basis of supporting the free world and America's position in the free world. ...

Question: At the two-day conference now being held on India, with Mr. Eric Johnston sponsoring it, the point has been made that India's present rate of progress is really not fast enough, particularly in view of the undeclared competition with Red China. ...

The President: Well, of course I have given a lot of thought to it, and everybody in this particular branch of Government has done the same. We have, after all, limited means. Now, we are a rich country and I believe that our—we will be richer as we are very generous, but very selective and very wise in the programs we adopt to help other countries, and one of these is India. But, since everybody wants more than you can give, you have got a problem that is never quite to be solved. I didn't know that Eric Johnston had a symposium on this matter but I know that everybody in the State Department, the ICA, Defense and everybody in that group in government is always interested in it, and I assure you this—I believe that India's progress should be more rapid, but I don't say that we have a sole responsibility to make sure it is.

Or on the subject of civil rights:

Question: Mr. President, I believe it was a week or so ago that you expressed your indignation over the kidnapping by a Mississippi mob of a Negro prisoner, and according to the news reports the FBI now has found the body. I wonder if, as you review this episode, that you feel that it emphasizes a need for stronger civil rights legislation. . . .

The President: Well I hadn't thought even about the idea that it needs new law in this particular case. The state authorities went on, got on the job immediately, they called in the FBI, they have been working in cooperation and law has been violated and I don't know how you can make law stronger except to have it, when you make certain that its violation will bring about punishment. Now I know the FBI is on the job and I have every confidence that they and the State Department—or, the state authorities will find some way of punishing the guilty, if they can find them.[9]

Yet Harding and Eisenhower were appealing, even magnetic political figures. In a reassessment of the Eisenhower years by liberals disenchanted with his successors, it has been suggested that his syntactical fuzziness was a calculated avoidance of direct answers to politically sensitive questions, and that in a general way his refusal to make sense reflected his determination to stay out of personal and partisan squabbles. Richard Nixon said of him, "He was a far more complex and devious man that most people realized, and in the best sense of those words."[10]

What the modern president lacks in the skills of speaking and writing, however, he can draw from the corps of communicators who work in and around the White House. Even a Franklin Roosevelt, who used words with zest and power, relied heavily on a stable of official and unofficial writers to achieve simple elegance and move a public dulled by the unrelieved banality of his Republican predecessors. His own public prose was stiff, but he knew how to guide and rework the writing of others to make it his. With their help he asked for public support and understanding and won it. Since Roosevelt, the public relations staff of the White House and press coverage of the president have grown considerably, and the ability of the president to present himself favorably to the public and to suppress unfavorable news has increased accordingly. These twin devices of suppression and glorification—with the faked opinion polls and faked messages from constituents of the 1972 reelection campaign of Richard Nixon as the logical limit—shape the popular image of incumbent presidents and candidates.

The Press As Intermediary

The men and women of the press engage in complex exchanges with their employers, with officials of the government, and with the public which keep them from being either too truthful or too untruthful. The hired help in the White House, and in advertising agencies during campaigns, work under no such constraints. Advertising agencies in particular are no more likely to respect standards of balance and integrity in merchandising the presidency than in their nonpolitical accounts—less likely, in fact, since the legal prohibitions on untruthfulness in advertising toothpaste and cereal do not affect "the selling of the president."[11] A good illustration of the advertising mind is Robert Goodman, whose accounts have included deodorants and Spiro Agnew simultaneously. He says, "We try to make the candidate bigger than life and we try to do it emotionally. Our job is to glamorize them and hide their weaknesses." Agnew, he exults, "was a beautiful, beautiful body, and we were selling sex."[12]

In a more down to earth way, presidents and their staffs have learned to reach the people through the press. Each medium has had its presidential pioneers. Theodore Roosevelt, at heart an exhibitionist, broke tradition by courting the press, providing an anteroom in the White House for reporters, and answering their questions while in the bathroom shaving and in other informal circumstances. Woodrow Wilson held more regular and more formal news conferences, and the press for its part learned to take some initiative in probing for news in the White House. In the twenties the presidency went into partial eclipse. Calvin Coolidge usually allowed no public mention of a press conference and no attribution to the president personally, but to "a White House spokesman" instead. He was not a newsmaker. Reporters occasionally wrote grossly inflated parodies of presidential remarks to turn their mouse into a more newsworthy lion. Under Herbert Hoover, relations between the press and the president cooled to a formality surpassed only by the imperial reserve of Charles de Gaulle in this century. From written questions submitted in advance by newsmen, President Hoover selected a number to answer. His rules allowed no follow-up questions or references in print to unanswered questions and assured his command of the dialogue.

After the drought, Franklin Roosevelt was as welcome to the press as he was to the people. In their enthusiasm, reporters drew him larger than life and he willingly played the part, until it lost its momentum in the late thirties, and he was revealed as a real man struggling with a refractory party. In his press conferences Roosevelt allowed attribution and a free exchange of questions and answers, with direct quotation by special permission. There were many conferences, some ninety a year on the average, compared with Hoover's sixteen.

It was radio that Franklin Roosevelt mastered, however, with unmatched flair. He was a patrician who spoke casually and concretely to an anxious public in time of depression and of war. In the first "fireside chat," in which he explained his reasons for ordering a bank holiday and asked the public to lend support, he set a high standard of rhetoric.

I want to talk for a few minutes with the people of the United States about banking—with the comparatively few who understand the mechanics of banking but more particularly with the overwhelming majority who use banks for the making of deposits and the drawing of checks. . . .

First of all let me state the simple fact that when you deposit money in a bank the bank does not put the money into a safe deposit vault. It invests your money in many different forms of credit—bonds, commercial paper, mortgages, and many other kinds of loans. In other words, the bank puts your money to work to keep the wheels of industry and of agriculture turning around. A comparatively small part of the money you put into the bank is kept in currency—an amount which in normal times is wholly sufficient to cover the cash needs of the average citizen. In other words, the total amount of all currency in the country is only a small fraction of the total deposits in all of the banks.

What, then, happened during the last few days of February and the first few days of March? Because of undermined confidence on the part of the public, there was a general rush by a large portion of our population to turn bank deposits into currency or gold—a rush so great that the soundest banks could not get enough to meet the demand. The reason for this was that on the spur of the moment it was, of course, impossible to sell perfectly sound assets of a bank and convert them into cash except at panic prices far below their real value. . . .

I do not promise you that every bank will be reopened or that individual losses will not be suffered, but there will be no losses that possibly could be avoided; and there would have been more and greater losses had we continued to drift. I can even promise you salvation for some at least of the sorely pressed banks. We shall be engaged not merely in reopening sound banks but in the creation of sound banks through reorganization.

> It has been wonderful for me to catch the note of confidence from all over the country. I can never be sufficiently grateful to the people for the loyal support they have given me in their acceptance of the judgment that has dictated our course. . . .
> We have provided the machinery to restore our financial system; it is up to you to support and make it work.
> It is your problem no less than it is mine. Together we cannot fail.[13]

It took a large staff to sort the mail the President received from an approving public in these first days of the New Deal.

Although they were poor public speakers, Harry Truman and Dwight Eisenhower carried forward the tradition of regular communication with the people: periodic news conferences and permission to publish the president's responses, paraphrased at first, then verbatim. John Kennedy thrived on news conferences and allowed the publication and broadcast of his responses without editing or delay. His success lay in a combination of charm and wit, which were his by nature, and thorough preparation for likely questions, the product of laborious briefings before each session, much as he had undertaken in his campaign debates with Richard Nixon. Kennedy's conferences made news and achieved a level of political entertainment well above anything the White House had provided in the fifties. Unlike Wilson and Franklin Roosevelt, Kennedy was unable to put his verbal skill to work moving the public or Congress, and he is remembered for intangibles—tone, style—and for his untimely death.

Neither Lyndon Johnson nor Richard Nixon liked the press. In Johnson's case it was a reflection of his loss of public favor, while in Nixon's it was an old feud between a professional politician and professional newsmen. In the wake of his defeat in the race for Governor of California in 1962, Nixon had sharp words for the press, who were, he thought, "so delighted that I've lost."

> Just think how much you're going to be missing. You won't have Nixon to kick around any more, because, gentlemen, this is my last press conference. . . . I hope that what I have said today will at least make . . . the press . . . recognize they have a right and a responsibility, if they're against a candidate, give him the shaft, but also recognize if they give him the shaft, put one lonely reporter on the campaign who will report what the candidate says now and then.[14]

As president, Nixon retreated from the rough and tumble of news conferences and restored the formality of the Hoover presidency. Like Hoover, Nixon preferred to confront the media on his own terms.

President Nixon felt more at ease and more effective speaking from a text than responding to questions, some unfriendly, in a televised news conference. Early in his administration he set a pattern of asking for free time to speak from the White House television studio on foreign and domestic policy disputes with Congress. Delivering a veto message or criticizing the Senate for rejection of a judicial nominee, the president could launch a partisan appeal to the people over the heads of his adversaries in both Congress and the press. Even this kind of appearance became infrequent, however, in his second term. His refusal to commit himself to a schedule of news conferences, even one a month, which would have been well under the twenty-four to thirty-six a year set by presidents Eisenhower, Kennedy, and Johnson, angered the press and dismayed the members of the public who either hoped to be informed or enjoyed witnessing his anxiety under questioning. President Nixon's avoidance of news conferences and his limits on subject matter in some elicited the organized protest of the news media.

Most questions at presidential press conferences are not hostile, and even a question of potential embarrassment to the president is easily evaded. Once recognized by the president, reporters usually ask questions they have polished and rehearsed rather than following up points raised by colleagues and answered inadequately by the president. Just how some teamwork can pin a president down, however, or at least expose his unwillingness to be candid, was shown by a rare series of blunt questions in a conference in President Nixon's first term.

Question: Mr. President, it's been about a month now since the May Day demonstrations, and in that period several people have raised the question as to whether the police handled it properly, and also the charges against, I think, more than 2,000 people arrested on that May Day have been dropped. I wonder . . . whether you think the police handled it properly, and the broader constitutional question involved of protecting individual rights in a difficult situation to control?

The President: Mr. Kaplow, yes, I believe the police in Washington did handle the question properly with the right combination of firmness and restraint in a very difficult situation.

Let us separate the question into what we're really dealing with.

First, there are demonstrators. The right to demonstrate is recognized and protected, and, incidentally, has been recognized and protected by the Washington police. Thousands of demonstrators have come down here peacefully and have not been, of course, bothered. They've been protected in that right.

But when people come in and slice tires, when they block traffic, when they make a trash bin out of Georgetown and other areas of the city, and when they terrorize innocent bystanders, they are not demonstrators, they are vandals and hoodlums and lawbreakers, and they should be treated as lawbreakers.

Now, as far as the police were concerned, they gave those who were in this particular area and who were engaging in these activities—approximately 15,000 in all—an opportunity to disperse. They did not. They said they were there to stop the government from operating.

I have pledged to keep this government going. I approve the action of the police in what they did. I supported it after they did it, and in the event that others come in, not to demonstrate for peace but to break the peace, the police will be supported by the president and by the attorney general in stopping that kind of activity.

This government's going to go forward and that kind of activity, which is not demonstration but vandalism, lawbreaking, is not going to be tolerated in this capital.

Three questions later a reporter returned to the subject of May Day.

Question: Regarding the mass arrests, I wonder, you seem to have thought that closing down the government, keeping it running in other words, was so important that some method of suspending constitutional rights was justified. Was it that important? Do you think it was?

The President: When you talk about suspending constitutional rights, that is really an exaggeration of what was done. What we are talking about here, basically, was a situation where masses of individuals did attempt to block traffic, did attempt to stop the government, they said in advance that's what they were going to do, they tried it, and they had to be stopped. They were stopped without injuries of any significance. They were stopped, I think, with a minimum amount of force and with a great deal of patience, and I must say that I think the police showed a great deal more concern for their rights than they showed for the rights of the people of Washington.

Question: If I may follow up, if that is true, then why are the courts releasing so many of the cases and many of the people that have been arrested? If they were lawfully and properly arrested, why are the courts putting them out?

The President: Because, as you know, that arrest does not mean that an individual is guilty. The whole constitutional system is one that provides that after arrest an individual has an opportunity for a trial. And in the event that the evidence is not presented which will convict him, he is released. I think that proves the very point that we have made.

Question: But they're not being released on the grounds that they— their guilt hasn't been proved—they're being released on the grounds that they weren't properly arrested.

The President: It seems to me that when we look at this whole situation, that we have to look at it in terms of what the police were confronted with when those who contended they were demonstrators but actually were lawbreakers came into Washington.

They were confronted with what could have been a very difficult crisis. They dealt with it. They dealt with it, it seems to me, with very great restraint and with necessary firmness.

I approve of what they did, and in the event that we have similar situations in the future, I hope that we can handle those situations as well as this was handled.

And I hope they can be handled that way—that well—in other cities, so that we do not have to resort to violence.[15]

At which point the president turned abruptly to the other side of the room to make it clear he wished to be given a new topic. Afterwards, when the president offered answers that were not responsive to newsmen's questions, no one caught him up, and the conference returned to normal with the president in control.

A minor embarrassment which may have contributed to Nixon's distaste for conferences is the occasional error of fact. The official edited transcript cleans up sentence structure—not the task it would have been in Eisenhower's day—and adds and subtracts in the manner of *Congressional Record,* which reports a genial approximation of the actual debate in the Senate and House. President Nixon's repeated confusion of South Vietnam and South Korea, for example, is missing from the official transcript; the length of the Laos-Thailand border once was corrected from 2,000 to 1,000 miles; the name of the senator from New York was changed from Goodwell to Goodell; the announcement of the capture of "small arms by the millions" in Cambodia became "small arms ammunition by the millions;" and so forth.[16] None of Nixon's errors occasioned the degree of misunderstanding caused by Harry Truman's reply, to a press conference question about the possibility of using nuclear weapons in Korea, that indeed nuclear weapons were always under consideration. People all over the world mistook an ambiguous statement about contingency planning for the announcement of a deadly shift in American war policy. Still, the likelihood of annoyance, if not acute embarrassment, may have helped induce President Nixon to keep the press at a distance.

It was critical commentary of television reporters following a presidential address on Vietnam that sparked the open war between White House and press late in the first year of the Nixon administration. The president's director of communications, Herbert Klein, perusing mail and telegrams arriving at the White House, sensed popular support for a counterattack. He passed his thought along to Vice-President Agnew, who opened fire on television reporters and shortly after on what he regarded as the newspapers of the eastern liberal establishment, while Klein himself disparaged press conferences.

> The essential purpose of news conferences is to transmit information from the president to the people. It was never intended to be a debate, or a show, or an arena for either the president—or the reporters—to show off skills or throw off animosities. . . .
> Let's face it: a presidential news conference—with 300 reporters clamoring for their moment on camera with 50 million viewers watching—is not the ideal format to reveal policy to world powers or to explain it in depth to the nation.[17]

According to one of the reporters under fire, "While most White House crowds develop a degree of paranoia about the press in time, this crowd began that way."

> But it was not out of spite that Mr. Nixon loosed the vice-president upon the press in the autumn of 1969. . . . He had carefully studied the Johnson "credibility gap," knew how fatal such a gap might prove for himself as he tried the exceedingly delicate operations of quitting a war without defeat and checking inflation without a depression. Dangers and setbacks were inevitable. What better way to avoid or postpone your own credibility gap than to impugn in advance the credibility of those who report and interpret your actions?
> The overall strategy was threefold: create public doubt that the reporters were treating you fairly; avoid direct meetings with them as far as possible; use television prime time as often as possible for unimpeded presentation of your case to the people.[18]

Nevertheless, polls indicated that the Nixon administration had credibility problems as serious as those of the Johnson administration before it. Neither president was given to candor and neither cared to submit to inquiries that might have restored trust. Certainly the suggestion that press conferences might offer public accountability through cross-examination of the chief executive, with follow-up questioning akin to the questions and supplementaries of the British House of Commons, would have been received coolly in the White House.

Along with presenting himself in the most favorable light, a president, by censorship and classification, can hide information that might jeopardize his popularity. There is always suspicion that information is withheld from the public less for reasons of the public interest and national security than to avoid embarrassment. In his concurring opinion in the Supreme Court decision which upheld the right of the *New York Times* to print the Pentagon Papers, the secret documents on the origins and enlargement of the war in Vietnam, Justice Douglas wrote, "The dominant purpose of the First Amendment was to prohibit the widespread practice of governmental suppression of embarrassing information.... Secrecy in government is fundamentally antidemocratic, perpetuating bureaucratic errors. Open debate and discussion of public issues are vital to our national health."[19] President Nixon and his attorney general argued that publication of the papers would do the United States "irreparable injury."

Even less secretive presidents attempt to manipulate and neutralize the press. John Kennedy planted questions in news conferences, insisted that the executive branch speak with one voice, stressed good news over bad, timed announcements for maximum impact, and once in a while asked newspapers not to publish damaging information unearthed by their reporters.[20] Just before the Bay of Pigs, he accepted the offer of *New York Times* and *New Republic* editors to suppress their correspondents' accurate accounts of American invasion plans. In Arthur Schlesinger's view, the press acceded patriotically to the president's wishes, "but in retrospect I have wondered whether, if the press had behaved irresponsibly, it would not have spared the country a disaster."[21] Kennedy's assistant secretary of defense for public affairs once described news as "part of the weaponry" of the government and asserted its "right, if necessary, to lie to save itself."[22]

In the Johnson administration, when the press was asked to suppress the story of the arrest of a presidential assistant on a morals charge, it declined.

If an adversary is making the news, and censorship is impossible, the president may attempt a diversion of public attention to the same general end. When Senator Fulbright's Foreign Relations Committee hearings on the conduct of the war attracted a large television audience in 1966, President Johnson made a sudden decision to launch a "peace offensive," flying to meet South Vietnamese officials in Honolulu. When Senator Robert Kennedy was about to address the Senate a year later to propose negotiation in Vietnam and a bombing halt in the North, Johnson delivered an unscheduled speech, called a news conference, announced an agreement with the Soviet Union to discuss arms limitations, produced hopeful statements on the war's progress from General Westmoreland and Secretary of State Rusk, and, when the talk had begun, released a letter to a sympathetic senator, Henry Jackson, defending the bombing program.[23] More recently Senator Jackson, as a candidate for the presidential nomination, on the verge of holding public hearings on the attractive issue of enlarging the Everglades park in Florida, was upstaged by an announcement from the White House that President Nixon planned a formal recommendation for the same purpose.[24]

Another technique of presidential news management is to allow or induce subordinates to attack the administration's adversaries without committing the president himself. The tendency to enlist vice-presidents in this work has been noted. Richard Nixon, who was given to this tactic and was himself a former hatchetman for President Eisenhower, responded to inquiries of newsmen in the wake of these onslaughts with assurances that the associates in question were expressing personal views. When Vice-President Agnew attacked the press, President Nixon's director of communications could describe him loftily as "a president who does not berate publishers or reporters."[25] While the president was restrained in references to critics, students, Democrats, and demonstrators, the vice-president escalated: "radic-libs," "effete snobs," and so on. And after top presidential assistant H. R. Haldeman described critics of the president's peace plans for Vietnam as traitors, in effect ("consciously aiding and abetting the enemy"), the president, as usual, would not issue a disavowal. He said that his critics might indeed impede negotiations with the enemy, although they were, of course, all honorable men. "I do not question the patriotism, I do not question the sincerity of people who disagree with me. . . ." Pressed to repudiate Haldeman's statement, the president would not.[26]

There is a popular will to believe extraordinary things about presidents, reinforced by a press that sides with the president to keep the public ill-informed of his activities, rare moments such as the Watergate disclosures aside. In exchange terms, the president provides the press with a steady stream of news of limited significance which the press sells to the public without major additions or deletions, a mutually rewarding relationship that is, in comparison with most of the president's, tight and stable. At the surface there are flourishes of controlled antagonism which belie the accord underneath, the inverse of the president's relationship with his cabinet, incidentally, which is cordial in appearance and typically tense in fact.

If a newspaper or television reporter ever had an urge to tell the whole truth and nothing but the truth as a result of conscience or a perceived public demand, and his superiors were compliant, the president would certainly retaliate in order to protect the traditional level of exchange. President Nixon acting through his subordinates regularly struck at transgressors in the communications media: the vice-president's attacks; Attorney General Mitchell's threats, later withdrawn under return fire, to subpoena the records of reporters who gave black militants undue coverage;[27] the FBI investigation of outspoken CBS correspondent Daniel Schorr, later implausibly explained by the White House as a routine security clearance for anyone under consideration for appointment to a high post in the executive; the campaign to terminate the licenses of unfriendly television stations and the funding of public television; the encouragement of grand juries to demand the sources of confidential information, with jail for newsmen who balked; and special audits of tax returns and wiretapping of investigative reporters. As it was, the crudity of the government's behavior only attracted another round of press criticism and delayed the restoration of calm. If it is the president who disturbs the customary relationship, newsmen respond with stepped-up criticism and independent newsgathering. Such was the reaction of the press to government censorship and war propaganda in the Johnson years.

The risks of upsetting the gentlemen's agreement outweigh the gains for both parties. Press and president offer each other public respect, comfort, and the prospect of continued employment. To break the agreement is to hazard the loss of a valuable resource. Few presidents care to invite a bad press, and few reporters on the White House beat want a falling out with the president.

There are a few stunning exceptions. The *Washington Post* persisted in digging for the facts in the Watergate affair in the face of White House efforts to discredit the stories and the newspaper itself. But the most daring journalistic coup of the decade, the publication of the Pentagon Papers by the *Times* and others, was after all a direct threat to the reputation of presidents who had retired or died, not to the incumbent. There is of course a good market for muckraking. Drew Pearson and Jack Anderson, his aide and successor, have based the most widely circulated column in America on exposés few of their colleagues would be willing or able to write. People come to Anderson for selfish or unselfish reasons with inside information embarrassing to public figures, presidents included, and he prints it. Anderson is the rare journalist, apart from the underground, who feels he can survive estranged from official news sources.

Most press assertions of independence and responsibility are not a vow to treat officials objectively as much as a determination to maintain rights of access within a closely cooperative system. When President Nixon eluded reporters in California once in 1970 for an evening in Los Angeles, the entourage of reporters and their editors were hurt and angry, not because they were missing a noteworthy event, but because their dependency had been disturbed.[28]

The net result of the transaction is to give the president a national audience for his views. Since his views are tipped in his own favor, the press itself helps to warm the romance between the president and the public, and this in turn leads to cycles of disillusionment—when the president fails to live up to the public's false expectations—and reconciliation.

Political Rewards for
the Public

The president's contribution to the ongoing exchange is twofold: political and psychological. The people stand to benefit objectively from governmental decisions in which he participates and subjectively by his presence as a symbol of authority and benevolence. Both functions are important, but at times they conflict.

Political rewards for the public depend on the president's ability to lead Congress, the executive, and the judiciary in making and implementing policy. These are relationships examined in other chapters. We may note that presidential policy leadership is valued by the people and is a medium of political exchange, yet opinion polls indicate that one might easily exaggerate the extent of public concern about, or awareness of, presidential policy leadership. Issues in particular are rarely as important in the public's assessment of presidents and presidential candidates as are personal characteristics and party affiliation. When issues are raised, the *appearance* of White House activity provides symbolic gratification for the public. A president who accomplishes a great deal may not be appreciated for it, and one who does little may enjoy public support and esteem.[29]

The psychic benefits bestowed on the people by a president do not depend significantly on good works. In contrast with the chief executive's political achievements, which are blunted by limited popular understanding and concern, they are inflated by a common tendency to invest the president—any president—with favorable qualities of authority and goodness.

Psychic Rewards for
Young People

The symbolism of the presidency is conspicuous in the psychic and political maturation of the average American from childhood on. We know from sampling attitudes about presidents living and dead, and most dramatically from responses to the assassination of John Kennedy, that presidents are important to children and adolescents. Children were deeply moved by President Kennedy's death and were expressive in the presence of pollsters. We can infer that he was important to them alive, too. For some young people the president and his family appeared to play oedipal roles: a boy identifies with the assassin and a girl expresses a belief that a woman was behind the killing, taking sides in the national tragedy in accordance with the fabled love competition in the family. (Comparably, a number of college students attempted to ward off vicarious involvement in the assassination by protesting that the president's widow could never remarry, a renunciation of their own affection in the guise of a universal taboo.[30])

Children in general shared the feelings of adults, a mixture of grief, shame, sympathy, and anger over the assassination. Children who were worried about the loss or departure of a parent were particularly moved by the tragedy which had befallen the Kennedy children. The older the child, too, the less his concern about taking harsh revenge upon the slayer, although teenagers often were studiously callous, flaunting their unwillingness to show emotion by repeating macabre jokes about the late president or showing annoyance at interruptions in social calendars and television programing in the period of mourning.

The assassination exposed interesting differences among young people by social class and, among college students, by course of study. Working class children were more likely than children of higher status families to express wishes for the punishment of the assassin, without regard for his civil liberties. Among college students, it was science majors, fraternity members, and athletes who proved the least distressed; the latter, however, had fantasies of elaborate tortures for Lee Harvey Oswald.

Sympathetic or aggressive, open or defensive, these responses depict the death of a president as a public event of unmatched private meaning to young people.

In happier moments the attitudes of children toward the president tend to be straightforwardly warm from a very early age, even before there is a rudimentary understanding of the office. A child in an elementary school is likely to see the president as powerful and benevolent—an honest, competent man who keeps peace in the world and does things for children. He is the center of the political universe, both awe-inspiring and personal.[31] Such an ideal develops differently in different children. In some it appears to be induced by the humane exercise of authority at home, from which the child generalizes. In others nearly the opposite takes place. Natural feelings of inferiority and vulnerability are exacerbated by parental harshness, and the child tries to compensate by telling himself that authority need not be threatening. He hides the unpleasantness of the authority he has experienced under a blanket of denials. It is the same kind of protesting too much that makes a pacifist of a man burdened with aggressive tendencies, or a prude of a lecher.

Children's idealization of authority is reinforced by saccharine accounts of the presidency in school, in books, and in most homes, while the president's remoteness makes it hard for children to test the generous assessments they have heard and read, and easy to project on him their personal attitudes toward authority. There are exceptions to these rules. One study found poor children in the hills of Kentucky less idealistic.[32] Instead of the usual complimentary responses, a group of boys and girls in grades five through twelve proved far less inclined than their urban fellows to regard the president as hard-working, honest, and capable. It is not clear whether the difference is largely a matter of geography, social class, or time, however. President Johnson was indeed suffering a decline in popularity in 1967, the year of the interviews.

After affect comes cognition: the child's typically warm regard for the president is complemented after a time by the first understanding of his work. The younger, more naive child may see the president as beneficent and all-powerful, the embodiment of government, who makes rules and carries them out with the assistance of his helpers in Congress. Still, surprising political sophistication was discovered in a study of Detroit children in grades four through twelve. The president was very much a political figure to the students interviewed. None of them was entirely misinformed, none described the president as performing services for children specifically, a clear difference from other samples, and in response to neutral open-ended questions about the president, they tended to volunteer concrete political information. Compared with the responses of adults, which fall short of perfection themselves, the children's were creditable. To them the president was more than a symbol of authority and benevolence or a substitute father; he was a real man facing problems of nuclear war, civil rights, and medical care. To these children the human qualities of a president were job-related, not the merely private ones of being a good husband or a good father. In this sample, at least, the difference between adult and youthful political sophistication was narrower than expected.[33] The children interviewed in Detroit seemed different from the Chicago and New Haven samples on which important earlier socialization studies had been based.

In another study, Canadian children responded differently in a key respect. They saw government not as the work of one man and his helpers, but as a team effort by Cabinet and Commons, as one might expect in a parliamentary system.[34] In this instance the question remains whether the difference was geographical or temporal, since the incumbent at the time of the interviews was the least colorful of recent prime ministers, Lester Pearson.

Attitudinal differences by sex and social class are more uniform. By fourth grade, boys give evidence of having greater interest in politics and more political information. Boys have normally been socialized to be more aggressive, and might well be attracted to an aggressive, competitive activity like politics and to a figure like the president. Family and companions of lower class children are more authoritarian, by and large, than those of middle- and upper-class children, and the children tend to be deferential toward authority and to idealize presidents irrespective of party. Authoritarians favor moral conservatism, strictness and punitiveness, and conformity to external authority, whereas middle- and upper-class parents value inquisitiveness, self-direction, and self-fulfillment more, giving less stress to the need to obey and conform. Middle- and upper-class families are more likely to explain the reasons for parental requirements and to permit children to discuss their validity.[35]

Despite all of these differences by time, place, sex, class, and age, the president remains the most likely central symbol of political authority for all American children. Most of them express warm feelings about the president very early in life, even before they have learned about his powers and functions. Broadly, the president is reassuring to them. It matters little to the children whether the qualities they like are real or imagined. Through him especially, the young are initiated into the political system as optimists, in ordinary times.

Psychic Rewards for Adults

On their way to becoming adults, young people acquire information about presidents that conflicts with childhood attitudes. For most of them the outcome is not the shedding of old attitudes so much as the adding of new ones to the old and a lifelong ambivalence toward the presidency. They retain much of their old idealism but gain a measure of realism or cynicism. Mixed feelings about political authority are a familiar phenomenon. An extreme case was the Aztec substitute king, a conscript whose fate it was to be worshipped and destroyed, living in splendor for a year and then slaughtered in a peculiarly unpleasant manner to make way for a new symbol of community fertility and vitality.[36] The difference in function between the Aztec king and the American president is a matter of degree. Polls in this country demonstrate that the typical American both distrusts and admires the president: he should be powerful, even to the point of overruling public opinion and Congress, but he must leave after eight years. The people are willing to ignore constitutional limits on presidential authority, in other words, but not on his term of office.[37]

The favorable side of American adults' attitudes about the president is seen in the response to a Gallup poll six months after the death of Franklin Roosevelt. Asked "Who is the greatest person living or dead in world history?" some 28 percent named Roosevelt, 19 percent Abraham Lincoln, and 15 percent Jesus. Incumbent presidents—capable or not—are nearly always at the top of the Gallup poll of the most admired living man in the world.[38]

Even allowing for ethnocentrism it is clear that adults, like children, hold presidents in high esteem and endow them with some attributes it is hard to believe they possess. A country without a monarch and ancient, sacred rituals may invest its politics in subtle ways with religious awe and reverence. Americans today are not as overtly religious as they once were, but they do have a religious sense of authority and the state. The easy meshing of the sacred and secular in popular thinking, particularly evident in the aftermath of the assassination of John Kennedy, lends the president a priestly quality, and in this the United States differs from most western democracies. A combination of intense and intolerant patriotism and a reverence for the presidency, especially in time of stress, gives American politics a religious flavor.[39] A president can pursue public favor by radiating religious imagery and ultimately, of course, by offering his life. Andrew Johnson was capable of suggesting both at once:

> If my blood is to be shed because I vindicate the Union . . . let an altar of the Union be erected, and then if necessary lay me upon it, and the blood that now animates my frame shall be poured out in a last libation as a tribute to the Union; and let the opponents of this government remember that when it is poured out the blood of the martyr will be the seed of the church.[40]

Religious allusions are standard fare in presidential rhetoric. Richard Nixon, for example, invoked God no less than five times in his first inaugural address in 1969, concluding:

> To a crisis of the spirit, we need an answer of the spirit. We can build a great cathedral of the spirit. We have endured a long night of the American spirit. But as our eyes catch the dimness of the first rays of dawn, let us not curse the remaining dark, let us gather the light.
> Our destiny offers not the cup of despair, but the chalice of opportunity.

The familiar ring, incidentally, is no accident. Nixon borrowed liberally from the impassioned rhetoric of another presidential address he admired profoundly, the Kennedy inaugural.

"Let this message be heard, by strong and weak alike . . ." (JFK: "Let the word go forth, to friend and foe alike.") "Let all nations know . . ." (JFK: "Let every nation know . . .") "Those who would be our adversaries, we invite to a peaceful competition." (JFK: "To those nations who would make themselves our adversary, we offer not a pledge but a request: that both sides begin anew the quest for peace.") "But to all those who would be tempted by weakness, let us leave no doubt that we will be as strong as we need to be, for as long as we need to be." (JFK: "We dare not tempt them with weakness, for only when our arms are strong beyond doubt can we be certain beyond doubt that they will never be employed.") "Without the people we can do nothing; with the people we can do everything." (JFK: "United, there is little we cannot do in a host of cooperative ventures. Divided, there is little we can do . . .") "Our destiny lies not in the stars but on earth itself, in our own hands . . ." (JFK: "Here on earth God's work must truly be our own . . . man holds in his mortal hands . . . .")[41]

People accept the view that presidents are not ordinary men. One evidence is their tendency to elect large men to office. In the 20th century, the taller of the two major party candidates for the presidency has won in almost every case.[42] Nearly all the contenders in recent years have been tall men—Hubert Humphrey at 5 feet 11 inches was among the shortest—and one hopeful, Edmund Muskie, equaled Abraham Lincoln's record 6 feet 4 inches. Experiments have shown that people impute height to those in authority, and lately it has been proven that in politics as in other walks of life people impute authority to tall men and prefer them for positions of responsibility. The perceptual distortions induced by people's need for symbols of authority feed on one another.

The public has a romantic view of past presidents too. There is a folklore—some of it true—of George Washington pitching a coin across the wide Potomac and confessing manfully to the felling of his father's cherry tree; of Abraham Lincoln studying law by firelight and splitting rails; and of Theodore Roosevelt leading a charge up San Juan Hill. Much of it is of interest mainly to children. But a modern adult mythology of the strong presidency—its emphasis on political rather than personal accomplishments, its hero Franklin Roosevelt—has largely replaced it in college texts and trade books. Authors sense a market for tales of presidential greatness, write books that raise popular expectations of their leaders, and thereby sustain the market for adulatory books.

The presidency in college textbooks often features Franklin Roosevelt leading the nation out of economic depression and personally assuring victory in war, Harry Truman courageously defending the land from communist encirclement, and General Eisenhower ending the war in Korea. According to this view of the presidency, the history of the country can be marked off in presidential eras such as the Hoover depression or the New Deal. Textbook presidents are teachers and preachers to the nation, active in the pursuit of national goals, and devoted to the use of federal authority in the service of justice and prosperity, while Harding, Coolidge, Hoover, and Eisenhower are given low marks for their performance. "What is needed, most texts imply, is a man with foresight to interpret the future and the personal strength to unite us, to steel our moral will, to move the country forward, and to make the country governable."[43]

Perhaps there will be a new textbook model one day. It is hard to predict. There was some disillusionment with vigor and initiative in the presidency in the late 1960s and the 1970s, however; and presidential reputations are more lightly made and unmade than one might suppose. The liberals' reassessment of the accomplishments of Presidents Eisenhower and Kennedy brought some of them to the official Republican view that Eisenhower was a prudent leader and John Kennedy a failure.

Whatever the incumbent's place in history is to be, popular writers tend to make him larger than life. Theodore H. White, in his best-selling series, *The Making of the President,* writes of the physical, perhaps spiritual, transformation of men who become president. Of John Kennedy: ". . . only his eyes had changed—very dark now, very grave, markedly more sunken and lined at the corners, than those of the candidate." Of Richard Nixon: "What was different was the movement of the body, the sound of the voice, the manner of speaking—for he was calm as I had never seen him before, as if peace had settled upon him."[44]

The mythologizing and overselling of the presidency has important consequences. The public, already disposed to think well of presidents, acquires such inflated expectations that disillusionment must follow in time. Rather than assess presidential performance straightforwardly, the public vacillates between favorable and unfavorable judgments—the way many people regard their parents, who never quite lose their better-than-human and worse-than-human character and are, therefore, both lovable and maddening in a special way.

Second, members of the public who desire to influence national policy-making will misplace their efforts if they attribute power to the president that in some cases is lodged in Congress or another part of the government. Third, distention of the presidential image inhibits the advisory function. White House intimates, far from being immune to the tendency to glorify the chief executive, are in fact some of the worst offenders. Honest criticism, which a president needs as a hedge against his own prejudices and the pressures of outside interests, does not come from a lackey.

And last, the overselling of the presidency may help induce a few mentally unbalanced people or rational, politically motivated assassins to make attempts on the president's life. The president is a symbol of benevolent authority to many, but for some he is the root of all political and personal problems. Nearly one president in five has been assassinated since Lincoln's time. The number of persons committed to St. Elizabeth's mental hospital in Washington, D.C., for threatening or other seriously disturbed behavior at the White House gates climbed steadily from about 10 a year in Truman's time to 120 annually in the Nixon administration.[45] Evidence is mounting that such behavior may be part of a deadly exchange, "a victim in search of an assassin." A president who defies fate may have an urge to be a victim, much as a drug addict, bank teller, or policeman invites his own occupational hazards. In many instances murder is provoked by belligerent or suicidal behavior. Three months before his assassination, presidential candidate Robert Kennedy said, "If anyone wants to kill me, it won't be difficult."[46] From the same period, Martin Luther King's prediction and acceptance of his own murder hours before it occurred is the explicit case, but presidents and candidates who expose themselves to throngs of people, knowing the risk, convey the same implicit message.

Assassination is the ultimate orgastic exchange of a president and the public, perhaps in some cases a kind of murder-suicide for the participants and for the spectators a cathartic political and religious rededication to the nation-church. Violent death and mourning uncover the passion in the relation between the public and the president. It is the explosive climax of a transaction that normally is carried on in a way that promotes the survival of both sides.

Deviant Cases

At the other less active end of the scale of presidential transactions are found the exchanges that have turned sour. The two best examples involve presidents who failed to sustain popular acclaim despite an inordinate need for it. Lyndon Johnson, like Woodrow Wilson before him, hungered for popular support and finished his term in office deserted by the public he had courted. The two presidents' undoubted talents as leaders were different. Wilson was at his best with a distant, abstract public, but inept in face-to-face exchanges with real people, while Johnson was the reverse, a negotiator par excellence and Lincolnesque teller of pointed tales in private, but not infrequently an object of ridicule in his roles of public speaker and ceremonial head of state. In the end both were lonely and equally unloved by the masses and close associates.

Each was to some extent the victim of the massive negative Lippmann described, the veto imposed from time to time on sustained, expensive international commitments by a tired and frustrated public. Public opinion may have been largely beyond presidential control in these moments. According to Lyndon Johnson, the people were above all prejudiced against Texans of humble origin.

> I had certain serious disadvantages which would ultimately preclude my ... completing my term as president. ... Those disadvantages I thought were upbringing in a poor setting, limited educational advantages, geography, where my mother was when I was born and the prejudices that exist, and in general, summed up in one sentence, a general inability to stimulate and inspire and unite all the people of the country. ...[47]

A more plausible explanation is that President Johnson pursued an increasingly unpopular course more and more rigidly as criticism mounted. The greater the criticism, the more confident he felt of the rightness of his war policy.

> People were here in the White House begging Lincoln to concede and to work out a deal with the Confederacy when word came of his victories. ... I think you know what Roosevelt went through, and President Wilson. ... We are going to have this criticism. ... No one likes war. All people love peace. ... But you can't have freedom without defending it. ... We are going to do whatever is necessary to do to see that the aggressor does not succeed.[48]

The president surrounded himself with men who were agreeable on basic issues and relied heavily on the advice of Walt Rostow, his assistant for national security affairs, an advisor who has been described as "exactly the wrong man for the job." The administration lost touch with the people.

Lyndon Johnson suffered more than his share of petty attacks. One has only to recall the popularity of *MacBird!*—a sadistic parody of *Macbeth*—starring a Lady MacBird who schemed to raise her husband to power by the murder of John Kennedy, thinly disguised as Ken O'Dunc. *MacBird!* was embraced by the young particularly, more out of pique at the president's country ways and his legitimate desire to move into the White House after the death of Kennedy than for his conduct in office. He also suffered the normal decline in presidential popularity as his term wore on. But Johnson was personally responsible for a good deal of his trouble with public opinion. He was inflexible in policy and too clever in his dealings with the people at large. The result was growing distrust—mutual distrust, doggedly escalated by the president in a manner that resembled the war policy itself.

The Pentagon Papers have shown in detail a duplicity in the White House long known in a general way by the people. A few days after the president and his advisors had concluded that air attacks would have to be launched against North Vietnam, for example—probably after a campaign in which he would maintain a stance of prudent restraint against the bellicosity of Barry Goldwater—Johnson said, "There are those who say, you ought to go north and drop bombs, to try to wipe out the supply lines. . . . We don't want our American boys to do the fighting for Asian boys. We don't want to get involved in a nation with 700 million people and get tied down in a land war in Asia."[49] The record is full of direct contradictions between internal and public policy statements on the war.

It was Woodrow Wilson's conviction that an alert, informed public was an asset to the president.

> The nation as a whole has chosen him, and is conscious that it has no other political spokesman. His is the only voice in national affairs. Let him once win the admiration and confidence of the country, and no other single force can withstand him, no combination of forces will easily overpower him. His position takes the imagination of the country. He is the representative of no constituency, but of the whole people. When he speaks in his true character, he speaks for no special interest. If he rightly interprets the national thought and boldly insists upon it, he is irresistible; and the country never feels the zest of action so much as when its president is of such insight and calibre. Its instinct is for unified action, and it craves a single leader. It is for this reason that it will often prefer to choose a man rather than a party. A president whom it trusts can not only lead it, but form it to his own views.[50]

Lyndon Johnson seems to have come to the opposite conclusion, that his success as president depended upon public ignorance and indifference. His successor, a more versatile politician, refused to concede the fight for public support as Johnson had. Like Johnson, President Nixon was handicapped by a poor public image, a critical press, and widespread distrust, but for a time he found a way of bypassing the press to appeal to the people directly, turning his secretiveness into a asset by exciting the public now and then with bold revelations, of which the news of his trip to China and wage and price controls were the most spectacular.

Conclusion

President Johnson's falling out with the public is the deviant case, while President Nixon's coming to terms with the public illustrates the norm: president and people need one another too much to be at odds very long. The exchange usually is intense, whether the president is a likeable Eisenhower or Kennedy or one less fortunately endowed. He may be a natural leader or have learned painfully by trial and error. But experience suggests that he will exploit the people's desire for visible political authority and leadership if he wishes to be counted among the successful.

Notes

[1]Theodore Lowi, *The End of Liberalism* (New York: W. W. Norton & Company, Inc., 1969), p. 183.

[2]*Congress and the Nation* (Washington, D.C.: Congressional Quarterly Service, 1969), II, 626.

[3]James David Barber, *The Presidential Character* (Englewood Cliffs, N.J.: Prentice-Hall, Inc., 1972), Chaps. 3, 6.

[4]*The Public Philosophy* (Boston: Little, Brown and Company, 1955), Chaps. 1, 2.

[5]John E. Mueller, "Presidential Popularity from Truman to Johnson," *American Political Science Review,* LXIV, No. 1 (1970), 18–34.

[6]"The Critic," *Time,* August 16, 1971, p. 8.

[7]Mueller, "Presidential Popularity," pp. 18–34.

[8]Dwight Macdonald, ed., *Parodies* (New York: Random House, Inc., 1960), p. 451.

[9]*Congressional Quarterly,* May 8, 1959, pp. 637–39.

[10]Murray Kempton, "The Underestimation of Dwight D. Eisenhower," *Esquire,* September, 1967, p. 108.

[11]See Joe McGinnis, *The Selling of the President* (New York: Trident Press, 1969).

[12]"The Selling of the Candidates 1970," *Newsweek,* October 19, 1970, pp. 36–37.

[13]Franklin D. Roosevelt, *On Our Way* (New York: The John Day Company, 1934), pp. 27–34.

[14]"California: Career's End," *Time,* November 16, 1962, p. 28.

[15]*New York Times,* June 2, 1971, p. 24.

[16]*New York Times,* June 11, 1970, p. 8.

[17] *New York Times,* December 29, 1970, p. 29. © 1970 by The New York Times Company. Reprinted by permission.

[18] Eric Sevareid in the *New York Times,* January 21, 1971, p. 35. © 1971 by The New York Times Company. Reprinted by permission.

[19] *New York Times* v. *U.S.,* 403 U.S. 713 (1971).

[20] Theodore C. Sorensen, *Kennedy* (New York: Harper & Row, Publishers, 1966), pp. 318–20.

[21] Arthur M. Schlesinger, Jr., *A Thousand Days* (Boston: Houghton Mifflin Company, 1965), p. 261.

[22] Sorensen, *Kennedy,* p. 321.

[23] Bruce Ladd, *Crisis in Credibility* (New York: New American Library, Inc., 1968), pp. 172–73.

[24] *New York Times,* November 24, 1971, p. 13.

[25] *New York Times,* December 29, 1970, p. 29.

[26] *New York Times,* February 11, 1972, p. 16.

[27] *New York Times,* February 6, 1970, p. 1.

[28] *New York Times,* August 3, 1970, p. 16.

[29] Mueller, "Presidential Popularity;" Philip E. Converse *et al.,* "Continuity and Change in American Politics," *American Political Science Review,* LXIII, No. 4 (1969), 1096–1101; Murray Edelman, *The Symbolic Uses of Politics* (Urbana: University of Illinois Press, 1964).

[30] Martha Wolfenstein and Gilbert Kliman, eds., *Children and the Death of a President* (Garden City, N.Y.: Doubleday & Company, Inc., 1965), esp. Chap. 6.

[31] Fred I. Greenstein, *Children and Politics* (New Haven: Yale University Press, 1965); Robert D. Hess and Judith V. Torney, *The Development of Political Attitudes in Children* (Chicago: Aldine Publishing Company, 1967), passim.

[32] Dean Jaros *et al.,* "The Malevolent Leader," *American Political Science Review,* LXII, No. 2 (1968), 564–75.

[33] Roberta Sigel, "The Image of a President," *American Political Science Review,* LXII, No. 1 (1968), 216–26.

[34] Jon H. Pammett, "The Development of Political Orientations in Canadian School Children," *Canadian Journal of Political Science,* IV, No. 1 (1971), 132–41.

[35] Greenstein, *Children and Politics,* pp. 92–93; Hess and Torney, *Development of Political Attitudes,* p. 224; Kenneth Langton, *Political Socialization* (New York: Oxford University Press, 1969), pp. 136–37.

[36] Harold Nicolson, *Kings, Courts and Monarchy* (New York: Simon & Schuster, Inc., 1962), pp. 17–19.

[37] Roberta Sigel, "Image of the American Presidency: Part II," *Midwest Journal of Political Science,* X, No. 1 (1966), 123–37.

[38] Mueller, "Presidential Popularity," p. 28; *Gallup Opinion Index,* January, 1972, p. 13.

[39]Sidney Verba, "The Kennedy Assassination and the Nature of Political Commitment," in *The Kennedy Assassination and the American Public,* eds. B. Greenberg and E. Parker (Stanford, Calif.: Stanford University Press, 1965), pp. 348–60.

[40]James David Barber, "Adult Identity and Presidential Style," *Daedalus,* Summer, 1968, p. 946.

[41]Gary Wills, *Nixon Agonistes* (New York: New American Library, Inc., 1971), pp. 368–69.

[42]"Heightism," *Time,* October 4, 1971, p. 64.

[43]Thomas E. Cronin, *The Textbook Presidency and Political Science,* a paper delivered at the annual meeting of the American Political Science Association, Los Angeles, September 7–12, 1970, reprinted in U.S., *Congressional Record,* 91st Cong., 2d sess., 1970, CXVI, Part 26, 34915.

[44]From *The Making of the President 1960* by Theodore H. White (New York: Atheneum, 1961). Copyright, ©, 1961, by Atheneum House, Inc. All rights reserved. And also from *The Making of the President 1968* by Theodore H. White (New York: Atheneum, 1969). Copyright, ©, 1969, by Theodore H. White, member of the Authors' League of America. All rights reserved.

[45]*Albuquerque Journal,* April 26, 1971.

[46]*Parade,* February 27, 1972, p. 2.

[47]*New York Times,* December 27, 1969, p. 8.

[48]Townsend Hoopes, *The Limits of Intervention* (New York: David McKay Co., Inc., 1969), p. 102.

[49]*New York Times,* June 20, 1971, Sec. 4, p. 1.

[50]Woodrow Wilson, *Constitutional Government in the United States* (New York: Columbia University Press, 1908), p. 68.

Seven

Summary and Conclusions

Presidential behavior resists generalization. High tragedy or low comedy, news of the day or history, it is a drama of unusual interest with an unpredictable leading man. But there are patterns in the story, we have seen, revealed by analyzing the opportunities for mutually profitable exchange between the White House and other parts of the political system. The closeness or remoteness in these relationships is better understood when we know what each participant will gain or lose by engaging in exchange.

In this light presidential behavior seems more stable. There are recognizable norms in the exchanges of presidents. And, of course, equally interesting transactions which deviate from the norms or do not fit a model of rational self-interest at all—political corruption of the magnitude of the Nixon era represents a risk-taking that is unlikely to appeal to rational politicians in the forseeable future.

With his party, the president or presidential candidate normally exchanges a will to win and the promise of policy leadership, patronage, and campaign assistance for election year support in the nomination and the election. His exchanges with advisors are more complex.

The norm in this case is a balanced assortment of close exchanges with advisors of different lengths of service and degrees of detachment from outside interests. The relationship of the White House and the bureaucracy in civilian programs tends to be distant, in contrast with an increasingly close and mutually rewarding entente with the bureaucracy in military programs. The president and the Supreme Court leave each other alone on important questions, typically, having rediscovered from time to time that they have little to offer one another but pain and embarrassment. With Congress the White House has reached an understanding that foreign and military affairs will be directed by the executive ultimately, and domestic affairs by the legislature. Finally, the president and the public have evolved a norm of intense exchange on two levels, the political and the psychological.

Exchange analysis suggests that James Madison and his fellow framers of the Constitution, with their vision of separated powers and checks and balances, have been vindicated by experience. It is precisely those components of the political system that were designed by the framers to compete and conflict—the president, Congress, and the courts—that are now remote and disinclined to exchange. Their transactions take the form of brief outbursts of mutual animosity followed by long periods of detente. The other parts of the political system, unanticipated by the framers, have been more adaptable to presidential needs, and he has been able to offer them a good deal in exchange. Parties as we know them began to develop soon after the adoption of the Constitution, but quite unexpectedly. The presidential advisory system is new, made and remade to suit the needs of modern chief executives. Even the public, as a political institution capable of transaction with the president, was unplanned. Indeed the Constitution in many respects was meant as a barrier to such an exchange. And the bureaucracy in military programs, in its present state a large, permanent, professional corps with both foreign and domestic functions, is entirely new.

In the legislative and judicial branches—Madisonian units of government—the president faces relatively independent and stable institutions not intended to cooperate closely with the executive branch. The other parts of the political system, with which the president can deal more effectively, have grown in influence on the bounty of exchanges with the president. The people as a political force, the party system, the advisory system, and the professional bureaucracy in military programs are all to a large extent creatures of the presidency; all are Hamiltonian rather than Madisonian institutions.

It will be interesting, and we shall hope not fatal, to witness whether the spirit of Madison or of Hamilton prevails in the long run. If exchange theory is valid, ambitious presidents are unlikely to expend much energy attempting to overcome Congress and the courts when they can improve their situation by devoting their attention to the extraconstitutional institutions with which exchanges are not inhibited by Madisonian constraints. It may be more profitable, from the president's point of view, to bypass and eventually to displace the less tractable constitutional institutions than to meet them head on.

Index